# E M BLAIKLOCK
## A Christian Scholar

# E M BLAIKLOCK
## A Christian Scholar

Trevor Shaw

HODDER AND STOUGHTON
LONDON   SYDNEY   AUCKLAND   TORONTO

**British Library Cataloguing in Publication Data**

Shaw, Trevor
  E. M. Blaiklock: a Christian scholar.
  1. Blaiklock, E. M.   2. Teachers – New
Zealand – Biography   3. Theologians –
New Zealand – Biography
I. Title
230'.092'4      LA2394.B59

ISBN 0 340 40253 9 Hbk
ISBN 0 340 40135 4 Pbk

Copyright © 1986 by Trevor Shaw. First printed 1986. All rights reserved. No part of this publication may be reproduced or transmitted in any form or by any means, electronic or mechanical, including photocopy, recording, or any information storage and retrieval system, without permission in writing from the publisher. Printed in Great Britain for Hodder and Stoughton Limited, Mill Road, Dunton Green, Sevenoaks, Kent by Richard Clay (The Chaucer Press) Limited. Photoset by Rowland Phototypesetting Limited, Bury St Edmunds, Suffolk. Hodder and Stoughton Editorial Office: 47 Bedford Square, London WC1B 3DP

# Contents

| | |
|---|---|
| *Acknowledgements* | 7 |
| *Preface* | 9 |

PART ONE: FROM BOYHOOD TO UNIVERSITY

| | | |
|---|---|---|
| 1 | Farm and school days in the Colony | 15 |
| 2 | Training college and conversion | 37 |
| 3 | Kathleen; and England revisited | 48 |

PART TWO: TWENTY-ONE YEARS TO THE PROFESSORSHIP

| | | |
|---|---|---|
| 4 | Lecturing and marriage | 71 |
| 5 | Career crisis | 87 |
| 6 | Journalism and a thesis | 96 |

PART THREE: TWENTY-ONE YEARS IN THE CHAIR

| | | |
|---|---|---|
| 7 | Living life to the full | 111 |
| 8 | Contending for the faith | 131 |
| 9 | Students show their appreciation | 142 |

PART FOUR: RETIREMENT YEARS

| | | |
|---|---|---|
| 10 | Blaiklock leads tour parties | 153 |
| 11 | Kathleen dies | 172 |

PART FIVE: FACING THE END

12  Active to the last                 183

Epilogue                               196


Appendix 1                             198
Appendix 2                             200

## Acknowledgements

For information on the early days of Professor Blaiklock, in particular when he was a boy on the Titirangi farm 'on the edge of civilisation', I have been most dependent on his several autobiographies. There are not many people from that scattered community of the first and second decades of this century, who can recall young Ted Blaiklock or who are alive today to do so. But Sidney and Janet Hesse are one couple from those early days whose help in capturing the spirit and incidents of those years has been most valuable. Another lifelong friend of the Professor, beginning from secondary school and training college days, to whom I am indebted, is Warnock Watson.

Other sources of information have been from the Professor's friends, associates and students over his long life of eighty years. All have been eager to speak of him and his contribution to their own lives. I have quoted at length from some of them. The contributions of others, from whom I have not quoted directly and who are too many to mention by name, have also been indispensable to me. And of course the Blaiklock family – Peter and Jean, David and granddaughter Alison, have been all that a biographer could expect in cooperation and encouragement.

There are three others who need particular mention. Alistair Paterson, after scanning the original material, made valuable comments. Ivan Moses, also advised on the original material, contributing significantly to a better end result.

And finally it was my son John Shaw whose editorial assistance in the final days of manuscript preparation was worthwhile and more than welcome.

*Preface*

Professor Blaiklock has been described as New Zealand's most popular scholar and best-known Christian. It was principally his books on religious topics (he wrote over seventy books altogether in his life) and his weekly newspaper articles over forty-one years under the pen name of Grammaticus, which gave him so widespread a popular following. In a *New Zealand Herald* article of 24 December 1985, Auckland Central Librarians named Blaiklock's books as still being the favourite ones in the religious section.

In his over 2000 Grammaticus articles, it would be difficult to name a topic on which he did not write. After his death the *Herald* published a selection of these articles, *The Best of Grammaticus*, and the book sold out its 5000 copies within a few weeks.

His ability to communicate to students was demonstrated by his honours students in his last year at the University of Auckland (1968) commemorating their studies with him by deciding to meet together every year on 21 September, the date of the birthday of the Roman emperor Augustus. They became known as the Augustani and met with the Professor every year from that time until a few weeks before his death in 1983.

Then there were members of tour parties he led to Middle East countries during his retirement, who also decided to commemorate the special knowledge and inspiration he had brought them by meeting together annually. The 1975 tour party held its tenth and final reunion in 1985.

Blaiklock's boyhood years are especially familiar to me. I was born eighteen years after Blaiklock and was also brought up on the edge of the Manukau Harbour, halfway between Green Bay and Blockhouse Bay, no more than two to three kilometres from the Blaiklock farm at Titirangi. The Mitchell home at Blockhouse Bay was also a familiar landmark for us even in my days – it was opposite the bus terminal where we gathered every day on our way to school.

Blaiklock lived almost his entire life in the one Auckland suburb of Titirangi. He moved into his Koromiko Road home in 1945 and until his retirement in 1968, travelled the seventeen kilometres to and from the university daily.

My first introduction to Blaiklock was in 1939, immediately before the Second World War, when he preached a sermon at the morning service in the Hamilton Baptist Church. Afterwards our paths crossed often, including one year under his lectureship in Greek and biblical history and literature at the University of Auckland.

In 1959 I was invited to the United States by the Evangelical Foundation of Dr Donald Grey Barnhouse, for a speaking tour on our literature work in Africa (my wife and I founded the Africa Challenge for the Sudan Interior Mission, 1950–53, and Envol Publications for the Congo Protestant Council, 1954–60). I was surprised and delighted on arriving in Philadelphia, to find Professor Blaiklock there, also having come from New Zealand to share in the Foundation's preaching circuit.

Particularly in the last year of his life, I was closely associated with him in the production of his television series (shown on New Zealand's Television One, after his death) entitled, *A Mind Behind It All*.

In compiling this story of Blaiklock's life, I have sought to portray him as I and a number of his close friends and associates knew him. The work is not therefore, strictly a biography but a biographical essay. In my research, I was able to draw on his own extensive library and his four autobiographies. Unfortunately, he kept very few records and files of his own manuscripts or personal and professional correspondence. There are many reviews of his books but only the favourable ones. Where there are notes and clippings, they are often undated and unsorted.

An intellect and a scholar, Blaiklock was able, in a period

of scepticism and liberalism, to reaffirm the authenticity of the earliest of the New Testament documents and the authority of the Bible. In effect, he gave Christians an intellectual and historical defence for their faith.

Trevor Shaw

# PART ONE:
# FROM BOYHOOD TO UNIVERSITY

# 1  FARM AND SCHOOL DAYS IN THE COLONY

The year 1909 did not begin as the happiest for the Birmingham family of Edward and Florence Blaiklock and their five-year-old son Ted. Edward was foreman of an electrical department of a local steam engineering firm. While the founder, Sir Richard Tangye lived, the family's livelihood was secure.

With the death of Sir Richard in 1908, however, his two sons took over the enterprise and soon decided there was no commercial future in electricity. The department was closed and Edward was without a job.

Then young Ted developed pneumonia. He became chilled to the bone while he waited in vain on a windswept corner on a cold, wintry Birmingham day for a friend who promised to play with him but did not turn up.

About this time also, a New Zealander crossed their paths and spoke in glowing terms of the climate and opportunities in that faraway colony. It was commonly agreed by those with some knowledge of the colonies, that 'the end of the world was good for children'. This their visitor confirmed and Edward began seriously to consider emigrating.

A romantic who delighted in tales of heroic endeavours at the frontier of the Empire, Edward had an ambition to restore the landed status which family tradition ascribed to his ancestors. As a youth he visited America twice, both times returning disillusioned with prospects there. Now Ted's sickness and the family's unexpected meeting with the New Zealander, came as pointers to their future. Edward and Florence reasoned it was a logical step to emigrate, as well as a way of escape from present problems for which they saw no immediate answers. Edward saw it also as the possible first step in the fulfilment of his life's dream.

There were other reasons why the appeal of New Zealand became irresistible. The young colony's long years of intense depression from 1879 to 1895 were followed by years of great prosperity in which land was readily available for new immigrants. Future prospects for those prepared to work hard were bright.

There had been a ten-year war with the indigenous people from 1861 to 1871 but fighting days were long since over. The Maori tribes were now specially represented in Parliament.

A Victorian Londoner by birth and nearing forty years of age, Edward did not find it easy to tear himself away. En route for Tilbury docks and before boarding the ship, the family paused a few days in London. It was a moving, emotional last look at the capital city for Edward and Florence but a trying experience for the six-year-old. Only recently recovered from pneumonia, he was forced to accompany them on foot over miles of London pavements. His protests at the ordeal were frequent and often shrill.

The Orient line, the *Otway*, was a new ship in June 1909, and in one of its four-berth cabins, the three Blaiklocks sailed from London. A call at Rome, the passage through the Suez Canal, stops in Colombo and Sydney all intrigued Ted.

At Sydney they changed to the *Mokoia*. Following a seasick voyage for Ted across the Tasman Sea, two weary months of travel finally ended. They disembarked at the port of Auckland. The town was built on a volcanic cone-dotted isthmus, the Waitemata Harbour on the east and the Manukau Harbour on the west. It was overlooked by the Waitakere Range, a wall of hills guarding its western flank and the Manukau Harbour, its southern flank.

It was midnight during a spell of fine August weather when they finally came down the gangway. They went to a hotel for the rest of the night and next morning found a cottage for themselves in Grey Lynn, a western suburb of Auckland. It was one of a small line of wooden houses with kauri tiles as roofing. Edward's seventy-five pounds worth of clinking gold sovereigns (part of the three hundred pounds worth he received from the sale of his Birmingham house), clinched the deal.

The typically English cottages were surrounded by little gardens filled with remnants of the pioneers' nostalgic shrubberies – privet, briar-rose and broom. A hawthorn hedge on the other side of the road hid the remnants of the town's first brickworks. Large weeping-willows shaded the back gardens.

As his parents settled in, Ted searched out his immediate neighbourhood. A little stream in the valley behind ran through a gorse and willow entanglement. Further down the hill, the dip became a ravine with tall gum trees on the slopes.

Ted loved to clamber among the gums, across the road to the start of Great North Road and down the hill to Western Springs. He loved the faint smell of the eucalyptus oil from the gums. By rubbing the green leaves together in his hands, he made it even more pungent.

The Great North Road ran to the frontier, somewhere in the bush beyond New Lynn. It was a great adventure for Ted to travel the several miles from town to this edge of civilisation. And it was here, on a raw wintry day in October 1910, that Edward and Ted went to inspect thirty acres (twelve hectares) of land Edward was considering purchasing at Titirangi.

The property's boundary could not be mistaken. It was where tree planting, and even cultivation itself, had ceased. On its east side a neighbour grew apple trees; to the south a copse of pines marked a cliff over the harbour; to the west were the steeply rising slopes of the Waitakere Range.

Evidence of the abuses of the early pioneers was clearly visible. Stumps of the magnificent kauri hardwood trees, unique to the northern half of the North Island, bore silent testimony to their having been destroyed in the previous century. Deep holes filled with dark, slimy water were legacies of the gumdiggers.

The stunted, starved bush was a clear warning to an experienced farm eye of the near impossibility of ever being able successfully to break in this land. Only in and around the swamp in the gully, did the shrub growth appear normal and the gully itself had long since become the receptacle for any topsoil the nearby land might once have had.

For a city worker from a country at the other end of the world, it was perhaps too much to expect that Edward could correctly interpret these signs. If their significance did penetrate his thinking at all, it was overshadowed by thoughts of his 'Great Estate'.

For Ted, the Titirangi acres all seemed a marvellous paradise. The fragrance of the cone-clustered pines which lined the road for two miles from New Lynn was a delightfully new sensation for him. The western hills across a wide, grey-green valley spoke of rugged strength and adventure potential. When he followed a well-worn track to the creek, he stumbled with glee on a sparkling stream with tiny trout and eels.

The stream originated in raupo swamps and flowed on two-thirds of the way down the farm to become the headwater of the Whau Estuary. Between the farm's western boundary and where the Waitakere Range ran into the tireless breakers of the Tasman Sea and the Manukau bar, only a handful of descendants of the early pioneers lived.

On a still night, it was possible to hear the moans and thunderings of the rollers pounding the west coast beaches miles away. It was a far cry from the busy Birmingham streets to the wilderness and isolation of the Titirangi farm nestled into the foot of the Waitakere Ranges.

With the inspection ended, the price agreed on and the precious sovereigns paid over, both father and son were well pleased with the purchase. For Ted, a whole new wonderland of mystery and magic was opening before him, ready and waiting to be explored, understood and conquered. For Edward, the establishment of the 'Great Estate' was now only a question of time.

The task, however, of creating a viable farm, complete with stately home, on hard clay was a dismal prospect for anyone, let alone an immigrant family with no farming experience. Others had tried before, some to grow wheat, all to give up and move to other areas.

Edward prided himself, however, on his good fortune in paying only ten pounds an acre. Just a mile and a half nearer the town, land cost four times as much – the difference between volcanic soil and clay!

There was now the task of building a home on the newly acquired property. Edward, handy with hammer and saw, took on the job of doing it himself, with the help of Florence at weekends. On weekdays Edward earned a living at the tramway maintenance depot in Jervois Road, Ponsonby, where his electrical experience was welcomed.

In Auckland, early pioneers had built big, stately homes with materials largely imported from the home country. Now these mansions were falling before the advance of commerce and industry. Consequently, demolition sites were not hard to find and builders' yards were full of materials suitable for the new home. On holidays and every available weekend, the horse and cart was filled with second-hand materials and the journey made from the Grey Lynn cottage to Titirangi.

Seated at the rear of the cart looking back towards the city, Ted found each two-hour journey a delight. He saw Great North Road lengthening and finally disappearing from view, passed the rocky wilderness of Western Springs, travelled through Waterview's avenue of pines bordering dairy and poultry farms and welcomed the clanging of the horses hoofs on loose planks as they crossed the Whau bridge.

On one occasion when they were on the way to the farm at Titirangi before the house was completed, Edward stopped the horse at the high point on the Avondale hills. The sun shone brightly from a calm, cloudless sky. Nothing interrupted the view of the valley below with its market gardens stretching to the tree and orchard-covered foothills. The blue wall of the Waitakeres stood out sharp and clear in a spotless atmosphere.

Turning to his son, Edward remarked: 'And some folk say there is no God!' It was more than a lesson in religion for the six-year-old. It was an experience of the reasonableness for the existence of a supreme being he was never to forget and always to be thankful for. It was also Edward's habit before leaving home in the morning for work, to place one hand on Blaiklock's head and say a short, brief prayer of a few words for his son's safety. Edward and Florence, however, were not regular churchgoers as the farm was too far away from a local church. Edward was a theist but both regarded themselves as Christians without pledging allegiance to any one particular denomination.

Edward was also a handyman, but he certainly did not follow orthodox construction methods. One of the 'finds' at a demolition yard was a magnificent, solid kauri gold Victorian front door. When its varnish was well polished, it shone like pale gold. All panels and pieces, it had a great brass knocker in the shape of a lion's head and a contemptuously lolling tongue.

Before the floor was laid or scaffolding for roof or walls erected, the door was securely put in place. Edward seemed to see no incongruity in a swinging door opening on emptiness and providing access to nowhere. The framework for the building was established around it.

Finally, after months of hard work and many two-hour trips to the site, the farm home neared completion and the family moved in. Two prized possessions brought all the way from Birmingham, contributed to the furnishings. A sectional oak bookcase held volumes of Dickens, Charles Reade and Wilkie Collins, along with Carlyle's *History of the French Revolution*, Bunyan, Shakespeare, a Bible and the *Colonists' Guide* and many others.

Every evening, Blaiklock senior, a self-educated man with a great respect for learning, would read aloud to his family from his small but select library. Favourite stories were Dickens' *Hard Times*, Thackeray's *The History of Henry Esmond*, Wilkie Collins' *The Woman in White*, Robert Louis Stevenson's *Treasure Island*, Rider Haggard's *King Solomon's Mines*, Bunyan's *Pilgrims Progress* and Defoe's *Robinson Crusoe*.

Ted was enthralled by the exciting adventures and stories unfolded to his young mind night after night. So much a part of family life did these stories become that it was commonplace for apt quotations to be made from them to one another during the day. As a result, by the time he started school, Ted's mind was already peopled with the characters from great literature.

Then there was the piano. In times of relaxation, Edward would sit for hours vamping and singing everything from 'The Mistletoe Bough' and 'The Vicar of Bray' to 'Abide With Me' and Negro spirituals he had learnt in the United States. Ted, however, was never attracted to the piano. His passion for reading left no room for any latent musical talent.

School days began for six-year-old Ted in 1910, at the Avondale South School, Blockhouse Bay. Superbly sited on a high point overlooking the Manukau Harbour, it was known as the Avondale 'side-school', an adjunct of the Avondale Primary School, two and a half miles away.

Ted had a walk of over a mile and the level of the stream running through the farm decided whether he stayed at home or went to school. There was no way to get to Blockhouse Bay other than to cross the stream. When the heavy rains came, the stream was almost instantly flooded. The roar of its gushing waters could be heard at the farmhouse.

There were many days at home for Ted in the winter months following his enrolment at the little side-school. But he was never at a loss for something to do. Settling down before the fire with a rug and the books his father had introduced him to, he could be content for the better part of the day. Arthur Mee's *Children's Encyclopaedia* was one of his favourites at that time.

Days at the school in Blockhouse Bay were not to last long. Both Ted's parents and those of his neighbourhood friend, George Strong, became concerned that in one of the sudden westerly storms that so often arose with little warning, the boys could be left marooned on the wrong side of the stream.

The next year, when Ted was in standard one, it was decided he should go to Avondale School. This solved the problem of the flooded stream but it meant a walk of three miles to the school and three miles home again. Ted and his friend joined a number of other children on their way along Astley Avenue and Portage Road. Lanes of pines dominated their route and they passed a large orchard on their way.

On one occasion an older boy in the group (Ted was then aged nine) distributed to each child one wax match from a box he carried. He suggested they strike them simultaneously on a stone and throw them into the tinder-dry brushwood. Quickly set alight, the ensuing fire sent black smoke billowing into the sky. It was clearly visible to all the school as the children lined up to march into their classrooms.

The next day at assembly, the headmaster asked who was responsible. The older boy in the group, without a moment's hesitation, admitted he himself was solely to blame. Neither Ted nor any of the others said a word and the older boy alone paid the penalty – a caning.

While at Avondale School, Ted's parents introduced him to the violin. He took lessons from a neighbour, about a mile away, using his mother's violin. On one occasion he was one of a number of children who had to 'perform' at a surprise party at a neighbour's home. He enjoyed the violin even less than the piano and was never asked to go through such an ordeal again.

In direct contrast to his delight in books, Ted found music practice, and particularly the violin, a boring chore. He lessened the agony by having a copy of the *Boys' Own Annual* or other tales opened on his knee. Listening adult ears could then be convinced, he reasoned, he was studiously continuing with his practice, when he was in reality engrossed in his reading.

On the farm one autumn day he searched out the source of the little stream that flowed through it. He had read of the discovery of the Nile River more than fifty years before. In making his way through his own miniature jungle – all kinds of trees, bushes, shrubs – he felt in harmony with the intrepid African explorers he had read about. He decided he would search as far as the Titirangi Road running along the top of the ridge and then make his way home.

Right under the ridge he stumbled on the spring from

which the stream originated. Not far from the source, at a point where it was richly lined with ferns, the stream divided into two. Following one arm he came on a pool in which he could see little trout swimming.

Then he noticed the two arms joined again with the crystal-clear waters completely surrounding a small knoll. Ted crossed to it. Fantails darted and turned and dived around his head. A young kauri tree flourished in the midst of the bush. It was all pure magic – an island resort all his own; a secret hiding place of which he vowed he would tell no one.

He was an only child and had no near-neighbourhood friend with whom to play regularly or to share his secret and he was far too sensitive to think of sharing it with his parents. On the rare occasion he took friends along the stream, he revealed his hideaway to none of them.

He built himself a wigwam which became his haven and refuge. This was particularly so when suffering from being humiliated or rejected at school, or upset by little unhappy events at home. At such times Ted always found relief in retreat, where natural surroundings and isolation brought peace and healing of spirit. The place was full of small, intimate noises – the chirp of insects, the eternal whisper of the wind and the sudden rush when a gust broke the barrier of the high black pines and bent the tops of the dry grass.

He spent many an hour there feeling utterly secure. After dreaming and meditating in summer hours, without fear of interruption and hearing only the sounds of nature and her creations, he always came away feeling stronger. Writing his autobiography forty years later, Blaiklock says it was in these times he first recognised a spirit of melancholia within him. It was a part of his character and throughout his life often became evident to close friends. It would throw him into deep despair, particularly when things were not going well for him.

Having finished standard three in 1913, Ted changed schools again, this time to New Lynn School. The advantage was in shorter travelling.

The summer of 1913–14 was an unusually dry one and burning off was common. On the farm, Edward was fighting a losing battle with gorse control. It defied all attempts to eradicate it. He cut an area of it, let it dry and then heaped it together in a pile with as much other growth as he could find. A huge bottle of kerosene was added and then a match to set it off. With a hiss and a roar, hungry flames quickly devoured the gorse and threatened to spread through the farm.

From his window in the house, Ted saw the smoke billowing high in the sky and then grasped the seriousness of the situation. There was nothing anyone could do but helplessly watch. Fortunately the blaze died down when the fire came to a well-beaten track near a farm boundary. But not before it had raced up the gully and seized on Ted's wigwam and the tinder-dry surrounding bush. His secret place was left a blackened scar. Having shared with no one his delight at finding the little knoll in the stream, he now endured alone his grief at the loss of his private sanctuary.

There were other incidents on the farm which made deep and lasting impressions on Ted. When five of the thirty acres were in grass, Edward bought his first three cows, two black and one a creamy Jersey. A fence was erected to keep them in but this proved unequal to the task. The cows got out and while Edward was at work and Ted at school; they made straight for the fat green leaves of the tutu plant in the gully. The tutu contains a powerful poison causing nausea and vomiting to adults and death to animals. The cows ate their fill and, with their stomachs starting to balloon, made their way back to the farm to die.

Edward and Ted worked late into that night – the former to strip the skins from the bloated carcasses. These could be sold and thus a little of the loss recouped. Ted's task was to hold the hurricane lamp for the skinning process and again as deep holes were dug for the cows to be buried in.

Ted's responsibilities on the farm, where required, and his devotion to his books, gave him little time to develop friendships with other pupils at New Lynn School. It is not easy finding contemporaries of his for the years 1914–16. One of them, however, is Janet Hesse (nee Knight) who remembers him as a very solemn boy who took little part in the usual childhood fun and games and no interest in girls. He accepted the rigid school discipline of those days and, she says, was even then regarded as being brilliant at his school work. There can be no doubt he was hardworking, attentive and generally well behaved in class throughout his primary school days. But there were times when even he rebelled.

In 1915, when he had turned twelve, his standard five teacher had a habit of keeping pupils in after school for a variety of reasons. They were free to go only when they answered five sums correctly. Ted had little difficulty in this area. Mathematics was one of his strong subjects. But on one Friday at the end of the second term, he became upset at what he considered was an unjust imposition, picked up his bag and fled from the church hall being used as a classroom.

His flight was noticed and the teacher ordered another pupil to go after him. Ted saw he was being chased. As he climbed a hill and began to slow down, he noticed the boy behind gaining on him. Slowing to a walk and now certain his pursuer would take him back to school, Ted was surprised when he shouted to him: 'Run on you fool, I'm getting away too!'

Back at school, the first day of the new term, both boys expected to be called to account. But not a word was said and the boys never learnt whether it was because the teacher forgave or forgot.

Ted appreciated the instruction and encouragement he received in standard six from the headmaster at New Lynn School. Mr Howard Ellis was a strict disciplinarian with a fiery temper who was never afraid to use the cane. He recognised Ted's intellectual ability and selected him and another boy living reasonably near Ted for extra lessons in his home two nights a week. These were to prepare them to sit the National Junior Scholarship examination at the end of the year.

Ted was prefect that year. Until then it had always been the practice of the headmaster to present the school prefect with a volume of the *Boys' Own Annual* at the end of the year. A lover of these stories he had read from a volume previously given to him, Ted looked forward keenly to winning his own volume at the end of the year.

To his chagrin, however, in December the headmaster announced a change of policy. Instead of the volume going to the prefect, it was from this year to go to the most popular boy in the school. Who that would be was to be decided by popular vote of the pupils.

It went to another boy in Ted's class – 'a skinny little fellow who could run like a hare and carried off all the firsts in the school races' as a disappointed Ted somewhat contemptuously remarked (Ted did not take part in school sports). It was a bitter pill to swallow from a man to whom in other respects Ted owed so much. Ted's father stepped into the breach and Ted was thus not deprived of a copy. But his father's gift did nothing to soothe the hurt he felt from his 'betrayal' as he regarded it, by the headmaster.

As a primary school pupil, Ted was a lonely boy who lived mostly to himself. As soon as school finished he set out on his long walk home. The hunger his father had awakened in him in good reading, he found, was not being satisfied at school and he hurried home to get back to his books.

Part of the journey to and from school was through dense bush on both sides of the road. On this part he walked alone, accompanied only by boyhood fears and imagined perils which found fertile soil in his vivid imagination. But it was not all imaginings. On one occasion he suddenly came face to face with a fierce-looking young bull glaring at him from the side of the road Ted was walking on. He immediately flung himself into the bush, alternately stumbling and crawling his way through until convinced the bull was not following.

But Ted had his own special farm friend. A few months before, Edward, while at the Westfield Meat Company saleyards, had noticed the sad look in the eyes of a horse whose working days were clearly over. To save his life, Edward bought him for ten shillings, named him Darkie and walked him home the many miles. Darkie became Ted and his friend's transport for some of their studies at night with the headmaster. With a rope around his nose and two sacks thrown across his bare back, Darkie made the journey much more pleasant for the two young students, as they studied hard for the National Junior Scholarship.

Many were the satisfying and sometimes exhilarating experiences at home for Ted during primary school days. His chores included wood gathering, helping milk the cows, making butter in the hand churn and delivering milk and cream to neighbours. He also enjoyed following behind the plough with a sugar-bag to pick up the unearthed kauri gum to sell to help pay the ploughman's costs.

The family lived on an excellent diet with their own dairy products, milk, butter, cream-cheese, abundant eggs and poultry and plenty of fruit and fresh, green vegetables.

Ted had a genuine love and respect for his parents, and the home environment was a peaceful one. But there were occasions when serious rows erupted. At these times Ted would generally take his father's side. They were 'workers together' on the farm and a real comradeship had developed between them even though Ted was still at primary school.

At the same time Ted recognised an overpowering attitude in his mother which he didn't like. And he was resentful of her, particularly over her occasional recriminations aimed at Edward because of farm failures.

As Blaiklock said goodbye to his mostly happy primary school days at the end of 1916, the World War with Germany had been in progress for two years. It contributed to a spirit of heaviness on the farm. But the war was not the only factor. In spite of years of hard work by all three, it was becoming increasingly obvious even to Ted that the hopes of his father for the farm were not being realised.

But now it was the question of which secondary school the young Blaiklock should be sent to in the new year. The emphasis at Seddon Memorial Technical College was on preparing students for business and commercial life. Auckland Grammar School was for those in pursuit of an academic career.

Blaiklock had some artistic ability and used a pencil well, which led his father to believe a technical training would suit him best. This thinking was influenced by his father's experience in the big Birmingham firm where he had envied the skills of the draughtsmen employed there and the security of their occupation.

Following Ted's sitting the National Junior Scholarship his father began to have second thoughts about secondary school. There was no question which school Ted preferred and finally his father agreed that if he won the scholarship, he could go to Auckland Grammar. If not, it would be Seddon Memorial Technical College.

For Ted, the holidays of 1916–17 were weeks of summer uncertainty. He never gave up hope. One evening he was in the midst of a game of dominoes at the home of a schoolboy friend. Scholarship results were due to be published any day. The father of his friend sat by the window reading the newspaper. Almost nonchalantly he turned to Ted: 'I see your name is in the paper. You seem to have won a scholarship.' Suppressing the strong emotion welling up within him, Ted replied in similar manner: 'Good', and continued playing. As soon as he could decently excuse himself and in a state of repressed excitement, he set out for home.

Along Godley Road, with darkness now approaching and no one near, Ted could no longer contain himself. He turned a few cartwheels, injecting a 'whoopee' or two in between. It was the only celebration of his achievement he was to enjoy.

Arriving home he found a parental crisis over a digestive problem of his baby brother, Jack, born only a few months earlier. So concerned were his parents they hardly seemed to hear his good news. If they did, they made little comment.

Ted resented his parents' preoccupation with his baby brother. The resentment was directed specifically at his mother, who from the time of brother Jack's arrival, seemed to Ted to direct so much of her time and affections to the new arrival.

In a more sombre mood, Ted continued to rejoice within himself. The die was cast. Uncertainty as to his future was over. All roads for him now led to Auckland Grammar School.

## FARM AND SCHOOL DAYS IN THE COLONY

Towards the end of January 1917, Ted set out to enrol at Auckland Grammar. The year before the school had moved from its building in Symonds Street (which became the arts building of the University of Auckland), to its majestic new site and building in Mountain Road.

Slipping quietly into the assembly hall, he was awed by the auspicious occasion. A tinge of anxiety seized him as he saw other boys being accompanied by one and sometimes both parents. He was on his own.

Ted didn't have long to wait for his name to be called by the headmaster, J W Tibbs. The piece of paper Blaiklock presented to him would have made him welcome at any secondary school. It was his National Junior Scholarship Certificate. Scanning it approvingly, Mr Tibbs said: 'Mathematician, eh? Of course you will be in 3A.' The third form classes ran to E and F.

Ted studied regularly and systematically at secondary school, determined to remain in the A forms. But life was a daily struggle for him. Mornings began early with the cows and there was his small milk delivery also. As well as giving him something to contribute to the family budget, the milk delivery also gave him money to spend each day at the tuck shop at school. It meant however, that he had to be early on his two-mile walk to catch the eight o'clock train at New Lynn. Each day he set out with a bag of school books on his back and two heavy twelve-pint cans of milk in his hands.

The evenings too, when previously his father had opened Ted's mind to the world of knowledge and books before the fire in the lamplight, now became a rarity. A baby brother in the house together with problems on the farm, made conditions at home difficult. Often at nights his long days resulted in his being almost too weary to take in lessons from Postgate's *Latin Primer* or Weekly's *French Grammar*.

Even so he found time to feed Darkie daily with warm bran from a bucket. The faithful horse would respond to Ted's banging on a kerosene tin as he heralded his meal time or, at weekends, a job to be done. Darkie signalled his response with his neighs and at meal times his thanks by nuzzling Ted's hands.

One afternoon Darkie failed to respond. There was no corresponding reply to the kerosene tin call. Ted went in search. An hour later he found him, his body firmly held in one of the deep holes left by the early gumdiggers. Only his head, neck and one foreleg protruded. It was impossible to dig the soil around him and ropes failed to free him; Darkie had to be destroyed.

Ted wept openly at so tragic a loss of his friend. It was 1917, his first year of Latin at Auckland Grammar School and as a monument to Darkie, he wrote on a board: MEUS HIC IACET EQUUS – 'Here lies my horse', and erected it over his final resting place.

It was in Ted's first year at Auckland Grammar that his father had a fall while working on the farm. He needed medical help. Ted knew a Dr Lindsay was that day visiting a family at Scroggie Hill, about three kilometres away.

He rushed to the house, waited until the doctor emerged and escorted him to the farm to attend his father. Ted also walked with the doctor on his way to catch the train back to town. Dr Lindsay urged him to consider medicine as a career. The idea struck in Ted's mind, remaining with him until the end of his secondary school.

Searching through Kealy's second-hand bookshop in town – it had become one of his favourite resorts – he found a medical booklet entitled *An Anatomy and Surgery of the Ear*. He bought it for sixpence.

The booklet appealed to him because at that time he was having hearing problems. From the back of the class where he sat in chemistry and physics, he could hardly hear the master. He knew something was wrong with his hearing but being very much a 'loner', consulted no one. He found in the sixpenny booklet, however, a possible diagnosis of his problem.

By worming his face round where he imagined the tubes were and several times inflating them by suddenly blocking a heavy exhalation, the tubes finally burst open. Normal hearing was immediately restored. This also helped confirm his desire to become a doctor.

But medical training required funds and this is what the family did not have. Ted's father at this time gave up his regular employment with the tramway depot to devote all his time to the farm. He believed he could earn enough from the farm alone to support his family.

In his second year at Auckland Grammar, Ted dropped history to concentrate on the 'basics' – English, two foreign languages, two sciences and mathematics. He ran into difficulties with mathematics, blaming poor classroom teaching for his low marks.

English was his delight, particularly under the tutorship of 'Porky' Mahon. He had been nicknamed years before Ted's time but he was obviously so called because of his being a 'thin and polished man'. Mahon had a major influence on Ted in three areas that were to become significant in his later life.

It was in Mahon's classroom where Ted began his public speaking career – he took part in a debate on the Roman Empire, speaking for ten minutes: 'I downed its imperial vices with fervour. Mahon's generous praise did my somewhat deflated person much good' (*Between the Valley and the Sea*, p. 79).

Blaiklock caught his first real glimpse of the world of classics through Mahon's readings from great English essayists: 'But the books we read – how they gripped my mind. Macaulay's Essay on Addison opened a new world for me. Under Mahon's tutelage I sensed what classicism in English prose meant' (*Between the Valley and the Sea*, p. 79).

Macaulay, the nineteenth century English essayist, described Joseph Addison (the seventeenth- and early eighteenth-century essayist) as 'the master of pure English eloquence'.

It was also Mahon's inspiration that led him to decide to study Greek for himself. It was following the reading of Pope's translation of *The Iliad* – the story of the war between Greece and Troy for the return of Helen – that Ted went out and bought his first second-hand Greek dictionary from Kealy's bookshop.

Mahon made me aware of another sort of English . . . He went further than essay. He bade us consider Pope's translation of the Iliad.

'May I be dead before that dreadful day
Enwrapped in robe of monumental clay . . .'
When all the Greek says is simply:
'Then me in death may the heaped-up earth be covering.'
(*Between the Valley and the Sea*, p. 79)

Through this indirect encounter with Greek and the classics, Ted glimpsed a future opening before him.

From this time also, Ted began a more serious reading of the Bible as literature. There was no searching for spiritual meaning, but the repetition of the words of the prayer read by the headmaster at assembly each morning did have its impact on him. They were '. . . and as we grow in our earthly knowledge, may we also grow in the knowledge of our Lord and Saviour Jesus Christ'. Ted understood and appreciated the first part of that prayer but the second part left him mystified.

Ted found the headmaster's reading out of the names of old boys killed in action, a sombre ritual. By 1916 the war had lost all of any crusading spirit it might have had for young people; for Blaiklock, death, even in battle for one's country, seemed such a waste of young life. He realised also that he and boys in his form could all eventually be involved in the conflict. Each Wednesday afternoon was set aside for compulsory military training. The shadow of possible eventual involvement in war hung over the heads of the boys.

In his first year, Ted, on a suggestion from his school friend Ronald A K Mason, was able to join the platoon of specialists – signallers whose duties freed them from the incessant parade ground marching up and down (on the school's big playing field). Being in 3A gave him immediate entry to this specialist squad.

Learning the Morse code was one of the requirements for the platoon. Practice was held in the quarry with one group signalling with flags to another some distance away. But the 'embryo' soldiers found it much easier to run unseen with their messages behind the wall near the quarry and deliver them by hand.

Sensing that his 'men' were not becoming as familiar

with the Morse code as they should, 'Dolly' Caradus (when he later moved to Mt Albert Grammar School he was re-nicknamed by the boys there as 'Granny'), the teacher in charge of the platoon, sprang a test on them. Unexpectedly he tapped out a message on the Morse code buzzer for the platoon to translate.

Caradus was the chemistry and physics teacher. When the message came through, Ted recognised enough of it to know it was a definition of an acid. He knew the definition by heart. Thus the platoon passed its test with flying colours!

Ted and Ronald also put their heads together regarding sports – another activity in which they were expected to participate. Both hated contact sports, particularly the mauling in the mud as in rugby football. They dismissed this latter sport (the most popular one in the school), as being for bodies more bovine than their own; cricket was assessed more favourably but required better bowling arms than either possessed.

In their third year, in 5A, they considered they had the advantage of the 'muddied oafs' in intelligence. They decided to study the art of running and rifle shooting. Perhaps, through their intelligence, they could create a reputation for themselves in these sports. A sprinter's advantage, they decided, came from a split second gained from the start line. But with no starter's pistol and no private place in which to practise away from derisive watchers they had no means of putting their findings to the test.

Ideas of rifle shooting research also ended when they found the Penrose rifle range was unavailable. Later, however, Ted became a proficient rifle shot, the ability remaining with him for life. (At the age of seventy-nine he could still put a bullet through an opossum's head at seventy-three metres.)

Eventually the two boys decided to direct their energies to launching a handwritten newsletter called *Searchlight*. In it they vented their eloquent scorn on 'mere muscle' and had their efforts promptly suppressed by their form master, E A Watkins.

As he considered the future, Ted recalled the remarks of his form teacher in his first days at Auckland Grammar: 'Most boys in this form will go through 4A, 5A, 6A and university.' For Ted it was not to be. In view of the financial plight of his parents how could he possibly contemplate 6A? He decided to apply to become a pupil-teacher, leading after two years to training college and qualification as a primary school teacher. He reluctantly accepted his qualifications fitted him for nothing else. It was not the end to secondary school years he envisaged or desired. But there was no alternative. He considered himself a failure.

His last attendance at Auckland Grammar as a pupil was for the end-of-year evening prize-giving. He would have loved to be receiving a prize himself, but even with his English, his marks fell just below the level necessary to win a volume of Shakespeare bound in heavy leather with the crest of the school on the cover.

After the prize-giving, Ted caught the 9.30 p.m. train from Mt Eden station and with a heavy spirit, tramped the two miles from the New Lynn flag-station home. The sighing of the winds in the pines fitted his mood perfectly and the morbid cries of the moreporks in the bush seemed the more penetratingly meaningful than he had ever before noticed.

Strongly in the grip of melancholia, Ted was unable to recognise that he was carrying away with him treasures far more valuable than the most expensive prize given that night. They were his love for language and literature, a fine appreciation of words and style and a deep-seated desire to strive for excellence.

The experiences of farm life and three years serious application to studying at Auckland Grammar had taught him that life was a challenge to be met by hard work and dedicated effort. Looking back in later years he would acknowledge that it would be difficult to devise circumstances that could have better equipped him for life. But tonight it was all gloom and despondency.

Farm finances were now in difficulties. With no regular weekly income since his father had given up his job at the tramways, they had fallen to their lowest level since their arrival in the country. Funding of studies to enable Ted to become a doctor was obviously out of the question.

At sixteen years of age, in 1919, Ted faced the future with deep misgivings. It was decided to sell the farm and Edward and Florence considered returning to England. Ted decided that if this became a reality, he would go with them.

The crushing disappointment for his parents was plain to see. With all the stern loyalty through these difficult days, Florence, despite her occasional upsets, stood by Edward throughout. But it had been obvious to her before Edward would admit it that they were battling against impossible circumstances. And it was Florence who pointed out, when the sale did eventuate, that the money from the sale of the farm, £1800, was equivalent only to what they would have had, had they, on arrival, banked their funds instead of pouring them into the hungry land.

Financially their years of toil and hardship had made them no better off. The monetary lesson was not lost on Ted. It gave him a loathing for debt, dependence and not owning what one used. As the year drew to its close, Ted was not sure which was the heavier blow – the loss of the farm or the closing of the door to him to medical training:

> I had some mightily difficult rough-hewing to do with my own future. I could see that the time had come when I must earn my living. My father was beaten by the farm. He sought escape from near-despair and planned, now the war was over, to sell all at the end of the year and return to England. No special plans were made for what I should do there. No one counselled me and the time came when I had to face some sort of personal decision . . .
>
> I was good at chemistry and pharmacy crossed my mind. I sought a position in a pharmacist's shop in those days and studied in the evenings at the Technical College. The prospect was not inviting save that I saw it as a possible back-door into medicine. I made a desultory attempt to find a position but that hurdle was not surmounted. No one wanted me . . .
>
> I felt I could not expect my parents to give up the dream of 'returning Home', and pay for a university course which could take me into secondary school teaching. I should therefore

have to begin 'pupil teaching', and train for work in a primary school.

(*Between the Valley and the Sea*, p. 84–86)

With the sale of the farm at the end of 1919, the family rented an old house on the cliffs above Green Bay. Edward went back to work for the tramways and his and Florence's return to England was permanently postponed. Ted, meanwhile, passed his matriculation and was accepted by Auckland Training College as a pupil-teacher.

## 2 TRAINING COLLEGE AND CONVERSION

The first Monday in February 1920, saw Blaiklock setting out for Avondale School in his new role. It was a hot day with a north-westerly wind blowing and high humidity. For the first time in his life he wore long trousers, part of a heavy suit which made him feel distinctly uncomfortable. The long walk to the school did not help.

His misgivings were increased at the school gate when a boy rushed up to greet him, called him by his Christian name and pointed him out to his friends. Blaiklock did not react. He was no longer just an older schoolboy from a Titirangi farm, he reasoned. He was now a pupil-teacher and between teacher and pupil there had to be a line of demarcation, surely.

Just how that was to be measured he was not sure but recognising the young lad as informally as he had greeted him was not appropriate. Blaiklock stared straight at the boy and without saying a word, walked into the school. The young boy stood in shocked amazement, certain his identification of Blaiklock had not been wrong but unable to understand why he should be so treated.

Four pupil-teachers were appointed to Avondale School: Blaiklock, another young man and two women. Blaiklock was sent to standard three, with its seventy pupils under the care of Miss Small.

He took his first lesson from *The Pacific Reader*, under the watchful eye of Miss Small. It was a lesson book he was familiar with. He emphasised the correct pronunciation for some children and posed one or two pertinent questions to test the understanding of others. Miss Small was obviously impressed.

She then informed Blaiklock she had to spend the next half hour with the headmaster. In her absence he was to give the class a history lesson, beginning in the year 55 BC. With a curt order to the children to sit up and an expressive glare that they could not fail to mistake as a warning to be on their best behaviour, Miss Small passed over responsibility and left the classroom.

Blaiklock was not expecting to be left on his own with the class on his first day. After his long walk from Green Bay he was tired. But he was ready for the test of his teaching ability. Noticing a tall stool in the corner he pulled it over and sat on it, twining one leg around it. It was an act of relaxation. The children also relaxed.

Blaiklock was confident in the subject given him to teach. He had just finished studiously working through an extract in Latin on Julius Caesar's reconnaissance across the English channel and of his war with the uncouth British charioteers. He had been particularly impressed with the standard-bearer of Caesar's Tenth Legion who had been first over the side as they landed on the shores of Britain.

Blaiklock drew a standard of a Roman legionary on the blackboard and spoke of life for a soldier in the army of Julius Caesar. He had no difficulty in filling in the time. The children were engrossed throughout. After twenty-five minutes Blaiklock realised Miss Small was due to return any minute. He unwound his leg, stood up, replaced the stool in the corner and ordered the class to sit up. Five minutes later Miss Small returned. Glancing quickly at the blackboard and then to a quiet, subdued class, she took over the reins of leadership.

No comment was made. None was needed. Blaiklock knew he had made a success of his first teaching assignment. He could handle children. More importantly, the experience convinced him that teaching was the career for him. All doubts were dispelled. His decision to start his working life as a pupil-teacher was vindicated. It had not been a mistake after all.

With a lighter step, he set out for home when school ended. Green Bay didn't seem so far away after all and his suit seemed less cumbersome than in the morning. A new door to life now opened before him and he determined to enter it with all the concentration and commitment he could muster.

Without realising it that day, Blaiklock had demonstrated to the large class of young children his greatest gift, one that in adult life was to win him thousands of eager seekers after his spoken and written words. It was the gift of being able to communicate simply and dramatically to people of all ages, deep truths and incidents from the classics and the Bible.

Blaiklock worked hard during the year but in October went down with measles. This prevented his having sufficient hours work in hygiene for a pass in that subject for his teachers D certificate. The required hours were made up when he completed a St John Ambulance first aid course during the summer vacation.

It had been a successful year for Blaiklock who was not required to do a second year as a pupil-teacher. He was accepted for training college for 1921-22.

> I found time that summer (1920-21) to turn back to the lordly Manukau, to literature, languages and Greek. Some plans were taking shape, secondary school teaching no less. Under my special pine tree on the cliff-top, from which I could see the whole indented coast down to Wood Bay, I thought much, read much and sought to find answers to some questions newly emerging and unresolved. I was seventeen in July and by that age, they say, most of us have asked all the questions we shall ever ask and perhaps found the rudiments of replies.
>
> I could see the rough places on the path ahead but that did not daunt me now I could discern a mountain-top. And I did see it, a very Everest. I intended to teach in the Auckland Grammar School, an ambition to hug close and communicate to no one.
>
> (*Between the Morning and the Afternoon*, p. 6)

While at Auckland Grammar, Blaiklock had begun a friendship with a fellow pupil, Warnock Watson, that was to last throughout life. They were together again at Auckland Training College, both pursuing a teaching career.

Warnock Watson describes Blaiklock in those days as a shy, aloof young man. To a casual acquaintance he gave the impression of being austere and lacking warmth. Blaiklock himself contributed to this by taking no part in the social or sporting life of the school and devoting himself entirely to his studies.

At home Blaiklock was no stranger to loneliness and built up his own private world around him. But he had two good friends with whom he often went boating on the Manukau Harbour.

Sidney Hesse was also an immigrant from England. When his own home broke up in the 'Old Country', he was sent as a boy to live with an aunt in Blockhouse Bay, Mrs Ada Patis. Also boarding with the aunt was another young man of similar age, Sidney Wood. They first met Blaiklock at a small Christian fellowship in Blockhouse Bay founded by the Abel family.

Sidney Hesse had a rowing boat which he moored at Blockhouse Bay beach. It was used by the trio for many excursions on the Manukau Harbour. The two Sidneys were disappointed, however, on the occasions when Blaiklock refused to go with them – his books and studies had always to take priority, he told them.

When he joined his friends on the water, Blaiklock thoroughly enjoyed the outings in the sturdy boat which lacked a centreboard and had an improvised brown sail. Together they explored the channels of the harbour as far along the coastal bays as Huia and across to Waiuku.

On Sunday afternoons of the last years of the decade, the three were often together at an informal Bible study led by Mrs Patis in her home. It was part of the Abel Fellowship, later to become the Green Bay Mission. Blaiklock enjoyed the company of other young people and participated freely in their wide-ranging discussions of world problems and solutions to them. It was a time of intellectual relaxation from his concentrated studies during the week.

However, he was not entirely in agreement with the two Sidneys when they planned, on a Saturday afternoon in May 1921, to go to the city for a special evening church meeting, but finally agreed.

## TRAINING COLLEGE AND CONVERSION

It was held in the Baptist Tabernacle at the top of Queen Street, a church struggling to become established. To boost its congregation, it had invited a young, aggressively evangelistic minister from Edinburgh, Rev Joseph Kemp, as its minister.

He appealed to young people in particular because of his forthright, direct preaching and the warmth of his personal conviction that in Jesus Christ only, were to be found answers to life. Blaiklock was impressed as he followed his address that night.

> Amid all my cultural enthusiasms and fulfilment, I sensed another dimension which I had not penetrated, something just a little beyond my reach. I was a theist. My deep romanticism aided there. I often thought about the vast Intelligence behind phenomena as I walked home under those thronging stars, the Pointers slanted inexorably by the immensities above me, for I had concluded that the mind which could think about them was a more marvellous reality than galaxies devoid of life. But it all puzzled me and there was no answer.
> (*Between the Morning and the Afternoon*, p. 16)

Kemp directed his message to the serious-minded, deep-thinking young persons with life before them. Deftly and persuasively he brought Christ and God and life together. God could be known and experienced in Jesus Christ, he claimed. 'Of course you cannot understand it all. You can only begin to do that by an act of acceptance, a commitment and an outworking of its meaning in the pattern of life,' he said. At the end of the sermon the preacher challenged any in the congregation who accepted the claims of Jesus Christ and were prepared to adjust their lives accordingly, to move from their seats and to stand with him in the pulpit.

Being a 'loner' from his earliest childhood and one who made major decisions only after long and careful deliberations, Blaiklock remained almost defiantly in his seat. The reasoned logic of the preacher he found acceptable. His emotionalism he rejected.

Casual comments about the meeting and the preacher passed between the young men as they made their way home. As was his habit, Blaiklock kept his deepest thoughts to himself. Only when on his own could he really weigh up the personal challenge of the preacher, which had impressed him.

Blaiklock felt no pressing burden of need on him. Fit and good looking, with waves in his hair and feet already on the first rung of the ladder to a teaching career, he was satisfied with life and its prospects. He decided to sleep on what he had heard and face the challenge of the preacher afresh in the morning.

The next day Blaiklock accepted that God was more than an abstract Intelligence behind creation and that he could be known personally in Jesus Christ. He took the step the preacher had recommended and committed his life to God in a simple prayer. He experienced a sense of release and settled peace within himself. He knew he was now a Christian.

At training college and university, in the early 1920s, a Christian was usually regarded as one who was unintellectual. Christianity was, in the popular view, for those who had failed in life or were opting out of it – a convenient garb hiding weaknesses and failures. There was also little public tolerance towards Christianity. The war with Germany had shattered old world confidence. Authority of all kinds was being questioned. Cynicism was rampant. A liberal philosophy dominated church theology. Christ was being reduced to a good man, perhaps the best of the race but a mistaken martyr; the Bible regarded as a book of poems and myths and religion as an outdated, irrelevant spent force.

Blaiklock was an adult in experience. He had faced some of the harsh circumstances of life and had learned that problems could not be solved by pretending they did not exist. He accepted that as he followed university life, he would be criticised for his Christian decision and even ridiculed. What he was not prepared to do, however, under the pretext of a misguided loyalty to his new life, was to close his mind to truth wherever he came upon it. He did not consider his decision for Christ gave him a cocoon of comfort into which he could crawl whenever faced with unpalatable facts. To withstand the pressures, his new experience would have to satisfy mind as well as emotion. He was to spend the rest of his life proving the historical authenticity of his new-found faith.

In practical terms, Blaiklock's becoming a Christian meant he had gone a step further than his father's theism and he had also won an acceptance into the warm Christian fellowship of the Baptist Tabernacle, whose services he sometimes attended when not worshipping at the Green Bay Mission.

Blaiklock found encouragement in his decision to become a Christian during the lectures at Auckland Training College of J W Shaw, Lecturer in English Literature and formerly minister of the Mt Eden Presbyterian Church (later named Greyfriars Church) and the readings recommended by him.

> I found a deeper integration in my studies, a unifying force in my wide reading. Some of my reading indeed, became intensely meaningful. Masefield's *Everlasting Mercy*, commended by J.W. Shaw as a most penetrating psychological study of conversion, completely fascinated me. The *'bolted door'* was indeed *'broken in'*. I knew the 'glory of the lighted mind'. I copied out in the library Francis Thompson's *Hound of Heaven*. The footfall had truly *'halted beside me'*. I knew what Christ meant by 'born again'. New forces, a new life, was most truly released.
> (*Between the Morning and the Afternoon*, p. 18)

These quotations confirmed Blaiklock's conversion experience and gave him an appropriate dramatic imagery to define it. God's mercy could never be changed – it was from 'everlasting to everlasting'. And when man fought against it by 'bolting the door' to his will, God's mercy would break down the door and enter. The 'Hound of Heaven' was God's Spirit who never gave up the pursuit of individual men and women, and he saw his own conversion experience aptly described as a 'footfall halting beside me' – the Holy Spirit of God coming alongside to help.

Blaiklock looked forward to learning more about teaching at training college in 1921–22. But the years were disappointing ones. The college taught students little new about practical teaching. Blaiklock found the lectures decidedly pedestrian and some of them repetitious from what he had learnt at Auckland Grammar School.

Students were required to attend lectures on subjects for the teachers certificates (they progressed from D to A) two or three days a week in Wellesley Street in the town. They were also permitted to take university lectures but the subjects had to be approved by the principal, H G Cousins. The latter decided how many university subjects could be taken on a student's capacity and his need. Education was obligatory. Blaiklock wanted to take French and Latin too. Cousins allowed him two only. He chose French and postponed Latin.

He determined to achieve a BA in three years but with the principal approving only two university subjects, he realised these might not be enough to ensure he achieved his goal within the time he had set for himself. Then he saw how he could do one more subject. Living at Titirangi, he was graded by the university as an external student. This meant he could sit the examination at the end of the year without attending lectures. Blaiklock accepted that his wide reading over the years would give him good chance of success, the English lecturer, J W Shaw taught from prescribed books and Anglo-Saxon should be within his reach.

When he was granted passes in three subjects at the end of the year, the principal called Blaiklock to his study. Why had he sat the English examination when the college had approved his taking only two subjects? Had he attended English lectures secretly? When Blaiklock explained his status as an external student, Cousins wanted to know how he had succeeded in passing. 'It is thanks to Swete's *Little Primer* and a habit of mine of memorising,' he replied. The principal was not impressed. He accused Blaiklock of being insubordinate.

During the year his friendship with Warnock Watson deepened, particularly following Blaiklock's conversion. Watson was also a Christian. Both shared their disappointment with college teaching. Looking back at the end of these years, they agreed the lectures theorising about child study, the history of education, school method and the like were wasted years. They would have much preferred longer time in schools gaining more experience in control and practical teaching.

Their greatest criticism they reserved for a book they were lectured on by its author, entitled *Democracy in the Schoolroom*. During sunny summer lunch-time hours under aged oak trees in Albert Park, they often discussed the new approach. The principles of this book could be successfully applied, they joked among themselves, where a classroom was full of angels without trace of original sin and the teacher a saint.

On the other hand, Blaiklock found real enjoyment listening to J W Shaw's sonorous yet expressive readings of the gems of English literature. These were fascinating sessions conducted by a man of enormously wide reading and culture. Shaw introduced him to Shakespeare, Milton and Marlowe, and to the world of modern poetry.

Poems were now added to the items Blaiklock carried with him to refer to and study during long hours of daily travel. Other items handy in his pocket were short lists of foreign language words, facts of history, dates, anything that contributed to the studies he was pursuing at the time. From an early age he had cultivated the secret and delight of memorisation and it stood him in good stead throughout his life.

When travelling into the city he had the choice of walking two miles from the cliff-top home at Green Bay to the New Lynn station, or a slightly shorter walk to catch the unique coach service from Blockhouse Bay.

The four-wheeled coach was led by four horses and driven by a local Blockhouse Bay character, Tommy Goulton. Passengers climbed into it by steps at the back and sat facing one another in two rows of about ten in each.

The coach took city-bound passengers to connect with the train at Avondale. The last part of the journey for the coach was up the hill to Avondale heights. Invariably it resulted in a race with the train chugging up the incline from St George's road-crossing at the same time. Tommy whipped the horses into their best performance as he strove to maintain his record of passengers never missing the morning 8.10 train.

As the train drew into the Avondale station platform, the galloping hooves came to a halt on the overhead bridge, the clatter of wheels on gravel ceased and from the interior of the coach the passengers hurriedly disembarked.

Watched by many eyes peering through the train windows, the passengers clutched their bags, cases or just-wrapped lunches, dashed down the ramp and into the carriages. As the last one sneaked in, the doors slammed shut, the stationmaster's whistle blew, the train puffed and steamed on its merry way and Tommy's record remained intact for at least another day.

Despite Blaiklock's reservations about the teacher training at Auckland Training College, academically speaking the years 1921-22 were ones of achievement. At training college, Blaiklock passed 'Teachers D' with recommended exemptions in four 'Teachers C' subjects – Education, General Hygiene, English and Psychology. At university in 1921 his BA subjects passed were English, Education and French; in 1922, Economics and Latin. A 'special report on student' from training college for the year 1922, and dated 8 January 1923, graded Blaiklock as follows: Academic, very good indeed; Personal, good; Professional, good.

With training college behind him, Blaiklock became a fully qualified school teacher for the start of 1923. For the first month he taught at Whitiora School in Hamilton, returning in March to Auckland to continue university studies. He was then appointed to Mt Albert School. He soon realised teaching such young children was not for him and he found the task burdensome. But he had to endure it for the rest of the year.

At university he studied languages and dug deep into medieval French. Some of the literary giants of the past had philosophies directly opposed to his own. He never shrank from their arguments or turned away from them. On the contrary, he made thorough examinations of their views.

A Latin poet and philosopher, Lucretius (c. 99-55 BC), attracted Blaiklock for the passion and power in his poetry. His name had come down through the centuries because of his poem *De Rerum Natura*, 'The Nature of Things', based on the atomic theories of Epicurus. Some trauma in childhood had made Lucretius desperately afraid of death. When he discovered the theories of the Greek philosopher Epicurus, that there could be no survival to disturb the soul, Lucretius became an instant convert. He grasped the doctrine with both hands and wrote his six books of poetry based on his new findings.

His philosophy was that the order and interlocking purpose we see all around, came about by a fortuitous congregating of atoms. To Blaiklock, this view needed a far stronger faith than his own, namely to believe that a great Intelligence had ordered it all. Lucretius was only one of the ancient scholars, the study of whom dominated Blaiklock's life at that time. But this was to change.

## 3 KATHLEEN; AND ENGLAND REVISITED

In 1923 Blaiklock found a new dimension in life apart altogether from his career, studies and his Christian faith. Halfway through the previous year, the Mitchell family, also migrants from England, had settled in Blockhouse Bay. They moved into a fine old kauri house at the highest point above the bay. It was the site of a fort in the previous century when Auckland was a frontier town in the land wars between the colonists and the Maoris. Practically the whole of the Manukau Harbour could be kept under view from this point.

Clifford Mitchell was a tall, thin youth about the same age as Blaiklock. In 1923 the two became firm friends after first meeting at the Green Bay Mission. Blaiklock introduced Cliff to the harbour, taught him to swim and took him camping at Wood Bay.

Cliff had a younger sister, Kathleen. It was not long before Blaiklock began to notice her good looks and gentle demeanour. Apart from a blue-eyed schoolgirl whom he had often noticed on the train when he was a student at Auckland Grammar School, he had never given much thought to the opposite sex. He was never given the opportunity to get to know the girl on the train or even to talk with her. For a brief period he had just adored her from afar.

It was the second time the Mitchells had emigrated to New Zealand from Kent. There they had lived in a lovely twelve-roomed brick house overlooking the Thames. It was a cosy home with large elm trees surrounding it and a vast barn. The family had a market garden, three farm cottages and employed a number of people.

After six weeks' journey by sea, the Mitchells had arrived in New Zealand for the first time in 1912. They became dairy farmers at Wayby, Northland. Their pioneering experience was never really successful.

When the older Mitchell boys left for the war in 1916, the father had to run the farm on his own. It was different from the farming he had been used to and he soon gave up and returned to England. With the danger of German submarines, the *Ruahine* carrying them back 'home' travelled via Cape Horn, making port calls at Montevideo and the Canary Islands.

Kathleen was glad to be back at the old Kent home which held such happy memories for her: animals to feed, elm trees to climb, strawberries and raspberries to eat, apples and pears to pick and, in the winter, thrilling toboggan slides over the snow and down the hill. Added to this now, was the excitement of the war. The home was on the direct route for enemy planes and Zeppelins flying to London with their bombs. On one occasion they witnessed a Zeppelin shot down in flames by one of the gunners from the ground.

Despite the war, these were idyllic days on the farm for the children. Kathleen was therefore devastated when she learnt her parents had decided to return again to New Zealand. She remembered all too well the hardships and the isolation of the early farming years at Wayby. She was now a leader at secondary school, all her friends were near her and she was being forced again to leave all this behind her. It would have been easier for her to have faced leaving had the earlier years in New Zealand been happier ones, or not happened at all.

When Blaiklock and Cliff Mitchell became friends, Kathleen was beginning to accept being back in the country and starting to recover from the hurt at having to say goodbye for ever to the Kent home. As she came to know Blaiklock she admired him but, to begin with, was elusive and withdrawn towards him. She did not want to risk another major disappointment in life.

The year saw their friendship grow and for Blaiklock, the achieving of his goal of a BA within three years. But he was unable to follow immediately with lectures for his MA degree (the degree he considered essential to become a secondary school teacher), until he had spent another year in Latin.

Money from the sale of the farm had now been received by his parents and they revived their earlier desire to return to England. They wanted to take him with them. He was, however, under bond to the New Zealand Education Department to give a number of years to teaching, and for both Blaiklock and his parents, breaking the bond was out of the question. They finally decided to visit England on an exploratory trip for a year only, taking their son with them, paying all his expenses as a reward for his work on the farm.

Blaiklock packed his Latin books for the journey. He thought about talking to Kathleen of what he now knew was his love for her, but finally did nothing about it. Both recognised individually that there was an attachment between them, but shyness and uncertainty as to how the other might respond kept them from broaching the subject. There the situation remained as Blaiklock, armed with his Latin text books, sailed with his parents on the *Ulimaroa* on the first part of their journey.

While the family were in London in early 1924, Blaiklock noticed an advertisement in the *Daily Express* for teachers. He had not really planned to teach while overseas and he did have his Latin examination to study for, but why not? He had his brand new teachers certificate with him.

At room 426 in the London County Council offices across Westminster Bridge, he was interviewed by a young man who regarded his documents suspiciously. He found it difficult to accept that New Zealand had qualified teachers. It was necessary to have the certificate authenticated, Blaiklock was told. He could do this only at the Education Department in Whitehall.

After crossing the foggy river, Blaiklock met an aged Education Department clerk. He kept the certificate for what seemed an interminable time, eventually returning it date stamped and initialled on the back. But the young man back in the county council office was still not satisfied. The date stamp and initial were not sufficient, he said. Blaiklock had to have a form signed by an appropriate Whitehall official which specifically said the certificate was genuine.

Annoyed at the response he received, Blaiklock only just managed to restrain himself from answering back angrily. He began, however, to have second thoughts. Turning back towards Whitehall, he stopped halfway across the bridge. Retaining his teachers certificate, he threw away the application form he had filled in and watched it float gently down to the river. He breathed a sigh of relief; after all, he had no real desire to teach the urchins of London County, he reasoned to himself. He had thought of doing so only as a way of gaining money so he did not have to call on his father's meagre supply. He had answered the advertisement on an impulse of the moment.

In a happier frame of mind and a freer spirit, Blaiklock watched for a minute or two as the river rolled its way to the sea, bearing his application form on its breast. Then he calmly walked away, glad to be distancing himself from a possible experience he didn't really want and one in which his impetuosity had very nearly embroiled him.

The family's next stop was Liverpool. Blaiklock had an introduction from the New Zealand Education Board and this he used to gain opportunities to speak on his adopted country to a number of schools in the area.

While there, his mother became ill and required some time to recuperate. With the help of an advance from her, Blaiklock decided to make for his birthplace, Birmingham. Securing good lodging in the city, he visited the university and grammar school. It was a nostalgic occasion. What if the family had never left for New Zealand – would he now be following an academic course at the local university, teaching at the grammar school or be a draughtsman at Tangye's engineering works?

After visiting an aged relative in Bewdley, Blaiklock found Fern Cottage, not far from Stanley Baldwin's home. He was enchanted by an area teeming with history. Fern Cottage, where he stayed for several weeks, had been a little inn on one of the pack trails which brought the Welsh wool on horseback through Wyre Forest to English markets.

It was springtime in an English countryside which had not changed for centuries. After the city experiences of London and Birmingham, the young New Zealander was delighted with the isolation. He took long walks to Dowles Brook and up the lovely Severn river to Arley. It was a time in which he could quietly reflect on his life – the hard, difficult years of farm life, school and training college when the tide of life seemed to be running against him. Then the turn of the tide with his BA degree, MA prospects just ahead and the prize of all, Kathleen and his love for her. They were not writing to each other while the Blaiklocks were overseas and he wondered how she was getting on thousands of miles away in New Zealand.

At Arley, Blaiklock came across an ancient church with a crusader in the nave and long grass among gravestones which had the names and dates largely eroded. The church was in a sleepy little village street. No one was about and only nature's creatures of birds, bees and the gentle blowing of the wind, encroached on the silence.

He remembered that the famous hymn writer, Frances Ridley Havergal had lived at Arley. Perhaps she had worshipped in this very church! Moving inside, Blaiklock entered an atmosphere of reverence and awe sanctified by centuries of devotion. As he knelt in prayer on one of the brown pews, the words of the famous hymn writer ran through his mind: 'Take my will and make it thine, it shall be no longer mine . . . Take my intellect and use, every power as thou shalt choose.'

Now nearly twenty-one years old, Blaiklock had been a Christian for three years. The experience had brought new meaning to life for him. In the silence and solemnity of that centuries old church,

> I thought . . . I prayed . . . of many matters and reached sharp-cut conclusions. I saw the need in those brown pews to be one with other Christians, that faith needed fellowship. I must join a church and not pursue religion alone. I drank tranquillity in great sweet draughts and realised what an earthquake, wind and fire so much of life had been . . . I seemed already to have lived a lifetime. I sensed a deep

surrender . . . I knew that any academic success I had had so far was incomplete and all dependent on sheer tenacity of work, but I knew too, that I could not maintain such intensity without that tranquillity of soul for which I was reaching. And that I seemed to find in the little Arley Church . . .
*(Between the Morning and the Afternoon*, p. 34)

There was no doubt he had Kathleen on his mind at this time. He was deeply in love with her, the only girl he had ever felt like this about.

Blaiklock had no family church tradition to uphold. His parents were Christian in the sense that most Britishers of that period were, but only in a very general sense. Kathleen, on the other hand, came from a different tradition. Her family was deeply religious and fundamental. Two brothers were ministers and a third, Cliff, was dedicated to becoming a missionary.

The 1920s in New Zealand were a period of social upheaval and insecurity for many. Unemployment was increasing and living standards being eroded by inflation. New Zealand still remained largely a conformist society. To win the hand in marriage of the young lady he loved, a youth had to be totally acceptable to the parents of his prospective bride. Without parental approval, there could be no marriage.

There was a sense too, in which Blaiklock felt Kathleen would make a real contribution to his life socially. He came from a working class family, she from the English gentry. Her parents would expect, if not demand, he reasoned, that he become a church member.

Blaiklock was a perfectionist. He had a genuine desire to be the best he could in everything he did in life. He was sincere in his dedication to God but there is no doubt that Kathleen played a large part in his decision.

The words of the hymn writer again, 'Take my life and let it be, consecrated Lord to thee', were far more than words to him. He expressed them audibly as he knelt alone in that little church in a deep, personal and private act of dedication of his life to God. On his return to New Zealand he would become a member of the Auckland Baptist

Tabernacle – and also seek the hand of Kathleen in marriage.

Blaiklock visited Paris, delighting himself, as he had done in London, in the historic places and buildings – the Louvre, Montmartre, Sacré Coeur, the Eiffel Tower, Les Invalides, Notre Dame. He discovered his New Zealand-acquired French did not equip him to converse with the local people. But he became encouraged about this grasp of the language when he met a Norman gendarme whose every word he was able to understand.

He would have liked to have spent time boarding with a French family but with spring merging into early summer and an examination to sit in Auckland in September, there was no time. But he did take the opportunity while in France to visit some of the famous battlefields of the war. He went on a guided tour of the Picardy battlefields, along the straight eighteen miles of Roman road to Albert, on to Bapaume and back in two wide eastern circles through Flers, Mametz, Thiepval, and Villers-Bretonneuz to Amiens.

During his years at Auckland Grammar School, the students had faced the prospect of their being dragged into the war machine themselves as they became of age. But this Sword of Damocles over their heads was removed when the war ended, at least for Blaiklock and his fellow students, in the latter half of his second year. He nevertheless still felt himself as having been involved, even though from a distance. Each morning in assembly at school, the head had read out the names of old boys from the school who had been killed in action, including the latter's own son.

On the battlefields Blaiklock visited there was still ample evidence of the ferocity of the war – shell holes, rusty wire, and the stark desolation. Blaiklock clambered down into one German dugout three storeys deep. It had been constructed to ensure the survival of its occupants. But on 1 July 1916 the occupants had all been found dead after a week-long bombardment by Allied guns.

The memories of this visit and the horrors of war stayed with him as he returned to England and to Kent. Here the Mitchell family had farmed, attended the local church and

## KATHLEEN; AND ENGLAND REVISITED

were still warmly remembered. It had been a long time for him without contact or word of Kathleen and, apprehensively, he wondered how she was.

One task remained for him to do. His upbringing had made him always conscious of the value of money. Determined to continue with his academic studies as far as he could go, he noticed a shop between the Strand and Trafalgar Square with masters' degrees gowns for sale. As the next year he hoped to complete his MA, he studied the price of the gowns at Whipples in Duncannon Street compared with prices in New Zealand. They were considerably cheaper and the gowns of excellent quality. He purchased one and true to the promise of the salesman, it lasted him throughout his whole academic career.

In England's mid-summer, the family turned homeward. Blaiklock still had to face his Latin examination. He had done the required translation, composition with his own readings of Vergil and Tacitus but there remained the prescribed books to read. This he planned to do after arriving home in the few weeks before the exam.

On the journey to England from Sydney he had enjoyed the company on the *Jervis Bay* of the Holt brothers, Lawrence and Horace, friends from Titirangi. Lawrence had commercial French to pass for a commerce degree and Blaiklock and another student who joined the ship at Melbourne, Geoff Green, took turns at reading to him from a French translation of Dickens' *Pickwick Papers*.

On the return voyage on the *Largs Bay*, however, there was no such comradeship for Blaiklock. The vessel carried hundreds of people emigrating to Australia. With their assisted passages, they were packed in wherever possible. They left few places on deck for solitude or quiet contemplation, but during the voyage he succeeded in closely reading George Eliot's novel *Romola*. While in a bookshop in London he had seen a copy of her novel on a shelf and remembered that JW Shaw had recommended it during his training college lectures. Blaiklock had bought it.

The story was based on Florence in the 1490s, the end of the first century of the Renaissance, when Europe was emerging from ecclesiastical and feudal despotism. In a great revival of learning, the Florentines rediscovered their classical Italian past. Feverish new thinking resulted as author after author and book after book, lost for centuries, came to light. From misty library shelves in half a dozen lands, the lost books of Rome and Italy became alive again in their native land. For seven centuries no Greek had been read in Florence. Now the Renaissance opened the door for an eager, hungry society to the overwhelming flood of newly discovered Greek thought.

There was another side to the Renaissance. Some regarded it only as a period of transition in which much of the good of the past was sacrificed and some of the evil retained. Italian society on the one hand exhibited an almost unexampled spectacle of literary, artistic and courtly refinement. On the other hand there were exhibited brutalities, lust, treasons, poisonings, assassinations and violence.

Political honesty ceased almost to have a name in Italy. Christian virtues were scorned by the foremost actors and ablest thinkers of the time. It fell to the Florentines to take on the historic task of reconciling the two forces of classical and Christian thought, making them relevant to their day.

From his pre-school days when the love of great literature and books had been so delicately and deliberately instilled into him by his father, Blaiklock had developed an unquenchable thirst to know more. In his early teens he had set a goal for himself of becoming a secondary school teacher and to this end his academic studies were essential stepping stones. But he was groping after something more. He had George Eliot to thank for bringing it all together and into focus for him.

From his reading of *Romola* he saw clearly the significant role the Florentines played at that crucial time in history. He began to feel a sympathy, even a kinship with them. On the return voyage from England, Blaiklock had many hours to absorb the lessons from the novel and contemplate them together with his own future.

He began to realise there were great literary and historical rewards to be reaped by digging deep into the literature of the Greek and Roman periods and the history of Palestine. He was beginning to see in outline his studies leading him to the foundations of European history and culture. *Romola* could have lessons and implications for the not altogether dissimilar conditions of the twentieth century.

In the biblical realm, Blaiklock was conversant with the inroads liberal theology was making into traditional Christian thinking. It taught that biblical writers of both Old and New Testaments had been conditioned by the times in which they lived, that there had been an evolution in the history of biblical religion. The Bible was being taught as belonging to the age of the coach, the bow and arrow, of sail and of tyranny.

The Bible had been stripped of its authority and from it modernists had exorcised any personal impact or relationship for the individual. Blaiklock regarded it as rationalism attempting to clothe itself in biblical garb. It was a challenge he felt compelled to face, if for no other reason than to satisfy his own intellect and personal experience of Christ.

At the same time, through the message of *Romola*, an awareness was being created within him that once again, at a crucial period in human history, there was a need for classical and Christian thought to be reconciled. Perhaps after all, the closed door to him for medical training had been in his best interests.

On arriving home, Blaiklock found his apprehension about Kathleen to have been unnecessary. The months of separation had confirmed in Kathleen her love for him. It seemed she had grown a little taller, and certainly had matured in that grace and beauty which had first drawn him to her.

A few weeks remained before his Latin examination and he made sure of his readiness by concentrated revision work. When it was over, he applied for a teaching position and was appointed to his old familiar school at Avondale.

Miss Small still taught standard three. Blaiklock was given standard five, relieving a teacher on long leave. He enjoyed the senior class and hoped he might get a permanent post with a similar class until he could complete his MA degree and then seek a secondary school appointment.

Blaiklock and Cliff Mitchell began the last week of the year by loading the boat with their tent and making for

Wood Bay. No house overlooked the bay, the tide reached to the edge of the bush; to the two young men, it was a world all their own. They retrieved the tent poles from the hiding place of the year before and set up camp in the snug, grassy corner by the lagoon behind the beach. It was an idyllic week for them both, although neither was aware at that time it was to be their last camping holiday together.

On the first day of 1925, Blaiklock rowed to Blockhouse Bay and picked up Kathleen. Returning to Wood Bay they walked together through the bush and sat down near the top over-looking the thick green forest surrounding the bay. It was the high point of a long friendship in which both pledged themselves to one another.

On the last of the incoming tide, Blaiklock rowed Kathleen back to Blockhouse Bay. A few minutes later he made for home again on the turning tide. As he rowed around Maori Lookout point and headed back to Wood Bay, he caught the last glimpse of Kathleen as she stood on the beach waving to him. Then the swiftly flowing current carried him quickly behind the point and she was hidden from view – but not from his mind or heart.

The fire was still smouldering by the tent as Blaiklock arrived back at Wood Bay. The young men decided to have an early night. But on his mattress of piled fern and tea-tree, Blaiklock found it difficult to sleep. His heart seemed as if it would burst from sheer joy.

Finally the elation began to subside and he experienced a deep, settled peace within as he surveyed the year ahead. It would be different for him than all others. Whatever the struggles (and he had faced many of these in previous years on his own), now he would have Kathleen with him.

The year promised to be a very full one in his studies. With a renewed commitment to the pursuit of academic excellence, Blaiklock looked forward to the challenge of sitting for his MA degree in Latin and French.

As the summer of 1924–25 lengthened and Blaiklock began preparing to return to his teaching position at Avondale School, the country entered one of its most disastrous years ever in the health of its young children. A severe epidemic of poliomyelitis struck. As the first day of

February 1925 dawned – the traditional start of the school year – it was decided children should not be congregated together for fear of spreading the disease. Schools were closed.

To give the teachers something to do, the Auckland Education Board arranged a series of afternoon lectures beginning in the middle of the month. They were to be held in the Kowhai Intermediate School at Kingsland. Blaiklock was not enthusiastic about such occasions. Even though the senior inspector was the principal lecturer, Blaiklock felt he would gain very little of value from them. But he went. It was a hot, muggy February day and he purposely made for a seat at the back of the lecture room. If he found the lecture to be as boring as he anticipated, he could read the booklet he had with him. Or alternatively, should he happen to doze off because of the heat, there was little chance of his being recognised from the platform.

As the senior inspector introduced himself, Blaiklock noticed a number of Education Department publications on a table behind him. Casually picking up the *Teachers Gazette* and flicking over its pages, his eyes alighted on the positions vacant section. Mt Albert Grammar School had a position for a teacher in senior French and Latin. Blaiklock could hardly believe his eyes! This was just the position to suit him, particularly with his sitting his MA in both subjects this year. To his horror, however, he noticed applications closed with the Grammar School Board at its city office at 4 p.m. that very day!

Unconcerned about the surprised look on the faces of the teachers next to him, he picked up his bag and was out of the door in a flash. He never learnt whether the senior inspector noticed him leave but his only concern now was to meet that four o'clock deadline. It was to be a race against time. Blaiklock had to get back to the house the family had occupied in New Lynn since they returned from their overseas visit, write out an application for the position, gather together the testimonials he had earlier decided might eventually come in handy and return to the inner city before the fateful hour struck.

Fortune seemed to be smiling on him. 'Pirate' buses had

recently taken to the streets in competition with the trams. Until laws against such practices could be framed and passed, there was nothing to stop them operating. As he ran out on to New North Road, one of them came along. Welcoming whatever fares it could find, it stopped at the signal of Blaiklock's hand. It was headed for New Lynn and twenty minutes later put him down a few steps from home. Hurriedly completing what he had to do, he rushed out for the next available bus to the city. It was not long in coming. With the hands on city clocks showing only minutes to four o'clock, Blaiklock deposited his application at the Grammar School Board's office in Shortland Street.

A few days later he received notification of an interview with the Mt Albert Grammar School headmaster, Frederick Gamble. Blaiklock remembered him from his own pupil days at Auckland Grammar where Gamble had then taught. A stern teacher of few words, 'Freddie' Gamble had a reputation for being a disciplinarian and Blaiklock wondered what kind of reception he would receive.

He was pleasantly surprised to find Gamble's attitude towards him was a kindly one and not at all as he had envisaged. Gamble assured him the position would be his and that it would be approved at the next board meeting. He would be given the lower sixth forms in both languages for ten periods a week. He would also itinerate from room to room teaching both languages to the third and fourth forms. It was a heavy schedule and he would not be required to be a form master.

With sixth formers only a few years younger than himself, Blaiklock realised the new appointment would be a real test of his teaching ability. Little had been said about discipline at training college and Blaiklock knew there was no magic formula for it. On the verge of achieving an ambition he had secretly guarded since being forced to give away hopes of becoming a doctor, he was determined to succeed in the unexpected opportunity now before him.

It was not long before he became confident that even with boys of nearly his own age, he was able to control and win their cooperation and confidence. Corporal punishment was an acceptable weapon in a teacher's disciplinary armoury. Occasionally Blaiklock resorted to it but when he caned one small youth much more severely than the latter deserved, Blaiklock was disgusted with himself and rarely resorted to it again.

By the time boys reach the sixth form, they have learnt that in direct confrontation with teachers, they invariably end up second best. This does not prevent them, however, from trying out the patience of new teachers in more subtle ways. Like every new teacher before him, Blaiklock had his test to face.

It came early, immediately following the first lesson he gave to one of the sixth forms. On returning to the common room at the end of the period, he discovered an apple core in his bag. At the start of the next period with this form, Blaiklock demanded to know the culprit. Slowly raising his hand and with a sheepish grin on his face, a prefect admitted his guilt. Having expressed disappointment at the prefect's conduct, Blaiklock offered him a choice – a caning in front of the class or reporting to the headmaster. The culprit was also given the lunch hour to make up his mind.

During the midday break, the prefect sought out Blaiklock in the common room. The latter suggested a third alternative: he would, he said, publicly apologise in front of the class. Hesitating a moment with his eyes fixed firmly on the youth and without a flicker of emotion or smile, Blaiklock replied: 'Let me suggest a fourth alternative – what say we both forget the whole incident!' It was never mentioned again, at least not to Blaiklock. But it certainly was among the members of that sixth form. A confrontation between their new teacher and a prefect was just too 'juicy' a situation for them not to be informed of the outcome. In their eyes, Blaiklock came through with flying colours.

It was not long before Blaiklock established a reputation as a firm but fair disciplinarian. And at the end of the year, as a measure of their respect for him, a number of sixth formers banded together and dined him at the Waverley Hotel.

It was this year that Blaiklock was unwittingly thrust into a position that gave him a place in the annals of Mt Albert Grammar School sporting history.

'Freddie' Gamble was as scornful as Blaiklock of the 'win-at-all costs' attitude in rugby football, particularly with the senior secondary school teams. He wanted the boys to benefit physically from any sport in which they were interested but was strongly opposed to the fanatical dedication which rugby demanded of its participants.

A recent group of immigrants from England had sons at Mt Albert Grammar and wanted their boys to play soccer which they themselves had enjoyed at schools in the 'homeland'. But soccer had not been introduced to any Auckland school – it was all rugby.

Gamble welcomed the request from the boys' parents and ordered Blaiklock to introduce it to the school. When the latter protested he knew nothing about the game, the head's curt reply was: 'Learn it, man!'

With the aid of a booklet on soccer rules and regulations and the cooperation of the boys and their fathers, Blaiklock quickly grasped the rudiments of the game. He also learnt there was a committee in Auckland trying without success to introduce the game to the city.

When this committee learnt that Mt Albert Grammar was introducing it to the school, its members were delighted. They quickly saw the wisdom of Blaiklock's advice that if it could be successfully introduced to secondary schools, the game would have an on-going pool of players on which to draw for the future. They gave Blaiklock their full support and also coopted him as a member of their committee. Blaiklock regarded it purely as one of the necessary jobs for a teacher and was later surprised to learn he was remembered as the one who introduced the code of soccer to the school.

In his studies during the year, Blaiklock became fascinated by the writings of two historians in particular. They were De Tocqueville and Tacitus. In much earlier years Blaiklock's father had introduced him to the French Revolution with its horrors. De Tocqueville filled in many of the gaps and some of his sociological theories, particularly on revolution, set Blaiklock thinking on the philosophy of history. The lecturer who enthused him with the works of the Roman historian, Tacitus, was Ronald Syme, later to win a knighthood as one of the generation's finest classicists and ancient historians.

Tacitus lived from AD 55 to the year 120, through the reigns of nine Roman emperors. He had no sympathy with the Epicurean doctrine and while he gave no clue to having any particular religious belief, his writings at times showed him to be a believer in a divine overruling providence.

In his *Life of Agricola* there is a sketch of conditions in Great Britain under the Romans; the concluding passage of the *Agricola* gives an account of the judicial murders of many of Rome's best citizens from AD 93 to 96. Himself a senator in those years, Tacitus felt almost a guilty complicity in the murders.

From his readings Blaiklock began to see history not just as a series of facts and dates to be learnt and digested but as a unity and a demonstration of moral laws based deep in the minds and ways of men; there was a wholeness about history and a oneness of the centuries. In their own periods, historical figures were becoming living personalities to him.

During 1925 Blaiklock also became interested in archaeology. Two events had awakened public interest in the subject. They were the discovery in 1922 of Pharaoh Tutenkhamen's tomb in the Egyptian Valley of the Kings and the publication in 1924 of the earlier volumes of the *Cambridge Ancient History*, outlining the successes of archaeology.

Blaiklock saw the benefit of keeping up-to-date with the subject and was more than justified in doing so as evidence from archaeology later came to be read alongside the literary record of ancient times.

Because of studying hard and Blaiklock helping his father on the farm as much as possible, he saw little of Kathleen during the year. But they corresponded with one another. Blaiklock always looked for a letter addressed to him in Kathleen's unmistakable handwriting on the common room table as the teachers gathered for morning tea each day.

In December of that year he made the most expensive

single purchase of his life – an engagement ring with three large diamonds, for Kathleen. Their engagement formally announced, they were in no hurry to marry. Kathleen had two years (1926–27) of training college ahead of her. They decided she should complete this first.

Following the decision he had made in the little church in Arley during his visit to England, Blaiklock threw in his lot with the Auckland Baptist Tabernacle. Joseph Kemp quickly recognised Blaiklock's gift with the young people of the church as they faced teenage frustrations and intellectual doubts.

On occasions Kemp stood down from the pulpit giving Blaiklock his first experiences in pulpit preaching. He delighted in the opportunity of being able effectively to pass on to others what he was finding for himself in his search for the integration of faith and knowledge.

During 1926 Kathleen developed a severe attack of mumps. Still sensitive to the world and insecure in himself, Blaiklock became apprehensive about the sickness. The last two years had gone well for him. They had been demanding ones, certainly, with his teaching and long hours of study, but the love of Kathleen added a new and happier side to his life, compared with his struggles in boyhood years. His sensitive nature and melancholia made him always wary of what life might do to him. Was Kathleen's sickness a sign that time was turning against him, that life was now to exact its payment for those two years of happiness and achievement?

Kathleen soon recovered but the experience was a reminder that he could never count on the pathway of life being clear and smooth for any lengthy period. Two lines of Lorenzo's poem for the days of the Florentine Renaissance seemed to fit his mood at this time:

> Who would happy, let him be,
> Of tomorrow is no certainty.

In November 1926, Kathleen received a letter from Blaiklock – the date stamped on the envelope was 9 November:

# KATHLEEN; AND ENGLAND REVISITED 65

Dear Kath:
Just a word to tell you that I will be up on Friday night. I think I can spare the time and it will be nice to have an evening together. You must excuse me not writing any more now dear and look forward to Friday. I've a lot to do tonight. Goodbye dear, Yours for ever, Ted.

So my little girl becomes my little woman today. God bless you sweetheart and keep you. Let us pray that your womanhood be one of joy and usefulness of help and happiness to me and that I be forever its help and stay. Look at the last verse in your daily light today. Your devoted lover, Ted.

Both paragraphs are written on the one page of the same letter.

As he grew into the fellowship of the Baptist Tabernacle, Blaiklock became increasingly aware of a great gap in conservative scholarship. He was immoveable in his belief that historic truth was as vital for a faith based on the Bible as was the correct interpretation of Latin and Greek writers.

For two years he had taught Latin at Mt Albert Grammar and had advanced considerably in his own Greek studies. But he realised he was not yet in a position to investigate literary and historical questionings of the Bible as deeply as he intended. But he saw it as an on-going task as his studies in the classics unfolded.

Apart from Saturday morning lectures with Professor A C Paterson, Blaiklock was rarely seen at other university lectures during the year. He was studying Latin and French for his MA as an out-of-town student and was not obliged to attend lectures. His teaching in the classrooms of Mt Albert Grammar gave him a fluency and a grasp of both subjects which only teaching can give. But he deliberately chose to attend Professor Paterson's lectures regularly. He found them inspiring and they became his introduction to the linguistic and humanistic approach to the classics.

In the few brief years left to him, Professor Paterson was to have an immense influence on Blaiklock's life and career. The thirteenth child of a Scottish Presbyterian minister, he was appointed Professor of Classics at Auckland University in 1924. In *Classics in Auckland*, published by the Department of Classics of the University of Auckland, and written by W F Richardson and L W A Crawley, Professor Paterson is described as follows:

> He was every inch the scholar – grave, learned and of dignified bearing. He had a pronounced sense of humour . . . was a marvellous linguist. He could speak English, French, German and High Dutch with fluency and was familiar with Latin, Greek, Hebrew and Sanskrit . . . In 1908 when the Transvaal University College was opened in Pretoria, he was appointed foundation professor of Latin, though at the start he virtually held also the chairs of Greek and German. In addition he gave lectures on Hebrew in the Divinity School. In 1916 he was appointed rector of the college and in 1918, when the university system of South Africa was completely re-organised, he was elected first chairman of the Senate of the University of South Africa . . . But the political undercurrents of life in South Africa in the 1920s eventually wore him down. It was clear to him that the Dutch wanted to convert the Transvaal University College into a Dutch university and were deliberately making things difficult for him as a result . . . Shortly after resigning all positions he happened to see the advertisement for the Chair of Classics at Auckland University and applied. When he was appointed, neither he nor his wife knew anything about Auckland. Even Cook's in Pretoria could not enlighten them. They tried the Encyclopedia Britannica but elicited only that the climate was wet. So when they arrived in Auckland in February 1924, with thirteen cases of books and three of clothes, they were indeed making a completely fresh start.

Blaiklock won first-class honours in Latin and French in 1925 and sat a second masters degree in Latin in 1926. With the Latin exam drawing near, he took a piece of Latin prose on Tacitus to Paterson for his criticism. The professor was impressed and urged him to apply for the vacant lectureship position in the Classics Department.

Previously aware of the vacant position, Blaiklock had shown no interest in it. It offered a salary considerably less than he was now receiving and he still believed his career was in secondary school teaching. He was also satisfied with his progress at Mt Albert Grammar, having convinced headmaster Gamble of his competence and ability. When the Grammar School became entitled to another permanent position, Blaiklock was appointed in spite of opposition from the Education Department.

Another disadvantage Blaiklock saw was that for a New Zealander, a lectureship at Auckland University would lead nowhere. Senior positions always went to overseas applicants. Appointing boards, still strongly influenced by the colonialist attitude, found difficulty in even considering applications for senior posts from New Zealanders. Blaiklock pointed out both objections to Paterson.

As with Gamble at Mt Albert Grammar, Paterson was impressed by the intellectual brilliance of the twenty-four-year-old Blaiklock. Paterson believed implicitly that in the long term, a university career would offer Blaiklock far greater scope than secondary school teaching. With the university desperately short of permanent lecturers of Blaiklock's ability, he set out to encourage him to apply.

Paterson impressed on Blaiklock that there was a limit to his own years in the university and that his time with the Classics Department could be even more limited. Auckland University, still part of the University of New Zealand, was already fighting for its autonomy. When that happened, Paterson confided in Blaiklock, he had been promised the position of the university's first vice-chancellor. To Blaiklock, he held out the possibility of two years' overseas study leave in the early 1930s.

If Blaiklock applied (and Paterson guaranteed that his application would be accepted) Paterson promised to guide him in his further studies and in the running of the department. When Paterson's time with the department eventually ended, Blaiklock would be qualified to step into his shoes.

For a young man it was a heady challenge which he could not dismiss out of hand, but Blaiklock had one further objection. When he had first enrolled at university in 1922, Blaiklock wanted to take Greek. But he was the only person applying for this subject. Paterson's predecessor, Professor Dettmann, had allowed Greek to lapse almost completely and refused to introduce a Greek course for one student. Although he had continued his own studies in Greek regularly (with the help of Paterson) Blaiklock explained he had no 'piece of paper' in the subject and this, surely, would go against his application being accepted.

Paterson knew of Blaiklock's ability in Greek as well as Latin and assured him that in his case, it would not count against him. As lecturer in the department, he would be required to manage Greek at first-year level and this Paterson was convinced, Blaiklock was well able to do.

Blaiklock left without committing himself but with Paterson's offer appealing more and more to him as he thought about it. The opportunity was indeed a very attractive one. But he needed to reassure himself about his ability in Greek, as well as time to think quietly about his decision. Arriving home he took Macaulay's *Essays* from the bookshelf, translated a page into Greek and returned next day with his effort to Paterson. It immediately won Paterson's approval.

Blaiklock now changed his goal in life from secondary school teaching at Auckland Grammar School to the university world. Paterson had convinced him he had the ability to succeed in this new field and Blaiklock pledged himself not to disappoint him.

On 26 November 1926, Blaiklock's photo appeared in the *New Zealand Herald* announcing his appointment as a lecturer in the Classics Department of Auckland University. It marked a turning of the page in his life.

# PART TWO:
# TWENTY-ONE YEARS TO THE PROFESSORSHIP

## 4 LECTURING AND MARRIAGE

The year 1927 saw Blaiklock give his first lecture at Auckland University in Room Two, the first Monday afternoon in March. Over the next forty-two years he was to utter millions of words in this room.

He had thoroughly prepared his first Latin lecture and spoke on Juvenal (Decimus Junius Juvenalis, AD 60 to after 128), the famous Roman satirist and poet. Blaiklock described him as 'that bitter old rebel who hated his mean garret in Flavian Rome, lashed out at all around him and lived to earn a pension from the Emperor Hadrian, lose his venom and conform' (*Between the Morning and the Afternoon*, p. 77).

When the hour ended, he found to his satisfaction that he still had ample material to spare. This did much to give him confidence in his own ability to hold the attention of eager, young university student minds.

From his experience at Mt Albert Grammar, he had already worked out his teaching methods, particularly in Latin. He put great emphasis on logic. He believed in turning an unseen translation, for example, into an exercise in logic. He would explain to his students how to isolate a unit of sense and then pass on to the theme. When a person's vocabulary failed, a verb could often give the clue to the meaning of a subject. As in a human body, he would explain, there are parts which vary in their essentialness; so too, there are parts of a sentence which are essential to its meaning. Even where some of the words are removed or not known, a core can be left which clearly gives the basic meaning.

Blaiklock's emphasis on logic was coupled with the need for diligent and systematic memorising of words. It was a sound foundation and the basis on which he began to build his long university career. His first Greek classes flourished and by 1930, the department had a full school of students up to honours level.

In the first year of his university life as lecturer, Blaiklock joined the Evangelical Union – the Auckland section of its national body, the Inter-Varsity Fellowship (IVF).

In universities throughout the world, the once powerful Student Christian Movement (SCM) was losing its old influence through the inroads of liberalism:

> This found its most foolish extravagances in the German universities where the very requirements of the Ph.D. degree pandered to irreverent, insincere and exhibitionist attacks on all tradition . . . The crossless Christianity, so common in the early years of this century, was the invention of Victorian liberals who were first daunted by the dogmatism of radical biblical scholarship. It was optimistic on evolutionary principles, turned Christ into a crusading knight, exploded its energy on social problems and for the more spiritually minded, substituted a personal mysticism for the lost authority of an inspired Bible.
> (*The Bible and I*, p. 33)

However, new groups of conservative Christians, standing for the authority and reliability of the Bible, were forming at many universities, including Auckland, under the Evangelical Union. Blaiklock regretted that the IVF had been compelled to separate from the SCM but nevertheless threw in his lot with the smaller group and helped the organisation become firmly established:

> It was not easy to identify myself with a small, intense group whom some found irritating and some amusing. The view certainly held by some 'academics' that nothing exists which they cannot see, hear, touch, smell or handle, always amazed me. It is odd that they do not realise that like any Christian, they exercise a faith. But the stand I took was intended to place myself unmistakably in the clear as a Christian, involving though it did, blame for any folly the students concerned might themselves commit. I accepted that responsibility.
> (*Between the Morning and the Afternoon*, p. 80)

Blaiklock had applied for an overseas study scholarship in 1926 while completing his second masters degree in Latin. He was still teaching at Mt Albert Grammar School and studying part-time. He was granted the scholarship in 1927 but by then he was in a dilemma about it. He did not want to disappoint Paterson by resigning after only one year of lecturing. And the decision whether to accept or not no longer concerned himself only – Kathleen and their future together had to be considered.

Kathleen had completed training college and was still under bond to the Education Department. Should he go overseas for two years study while Kathleen completed her bond? Should they marry now, and Kathleen accompany him overseas? If so, what about having to pay back the bond and also their own living costs while overseas? The scholarship would not cover their daily living costs. Austere childhood days had left them both very security-minded and there was no guarantee that if Kathleen accompanied him, she would find work in England.

Kathleen made no attempt to influence Blaiklock. She considered it was his decision alone and she would be content whatever it was. They talked it over fully together and also prayed about it.

A big factor in Blaiklock's decision was the confidence he had in the prospects Professor Paterson was holding out to him within the Classics Department. There was little doubt he planned to groom Blaiklock for a senior position and the latter knew he could receive no better training than under Paterson's scholarship.

Blaiklock and Kathleen's caution over finances and Paterson's promises of better things to come led Blaiklock to reject the postgraduate scholarship. A few years later they were to regret having made this decision but at the time, they both expressed having a deep inner peace about it, believing it to be the right one.

Blaiklock and Kathleen decided there was no reason to delay marriage any longer. It was over five years since the Mitchell family had returned to New Zealand and over four years since Cliff Mitchell's younger sister had begun to have meaning in Blaiklock's life. It was two years since they had pledged each to the other on that summer day on the bushclad slopes overlooking Wood Bay. They decided not to accept the scholarship and planned their wedding for January 1928. But it was not to be.

Edward and Florence Blaiklock had long been undecided about when they should return to England. Having failed on the Titirangi farm and becoming weary of life back in the electrical repair barn of the tramways, Edward was determined to make one more effort to prove he could farm successfully. He finally decided to return 'home' and take up chicken farming in the West Country.

Blaiklock agreed to use some of the money from the sale of his parent's house to help finance the home he was buying for their marriage in Weston Avenue on the northwest slopes of Mt Albert with its views to Titirangi and the Waitakere Ranges. Edward and Florence would then have at least some of their remaining capital safely invested.

The parents moved into the Weston Avenue house, originally for just a short period before their departure for England. It cost Blaiklock £1750. A year later, when the worldwide recession had really begun to bite in New Zealand, its market value fell to £500.

Edward senior continued to suffer crises of indecision about returning to England and delays were also experienced with enquiries and agencies in the 'Old Country'. To allow his parents to stay in the house until their departure, Blaiklock postponed the marriage. It finally took place on 13 November 1928 at the Auckland Baptist Tabernacle:

> Our chosen day (November 14) was commandeered by the Government for an election – the occasion when the United Party intruded and disrupted the whole scene of things. That merely made us step back one day, having no superstitious fears of the thirteenth. We gathered, hardly more than our own family . . .
>
> (*Between the Morning and the Afternoon*, p. 91)

The wedding breakfast was held in the kiosk on the slopes of Mt Eden, opened only six weeks previously. An extinct volcano, Mt Eden is Auckland's highest peak with expansive views of the city, both harbours and the

Waitakeres. With its beautiful kiosk gardens, it has remained one of the city's most picturesque spots. The newlyweds spent their honeymoon at the thermal district of Rotorua in the centre of the North Island.

For the first anniversary of their marriage in November 1929, they celebrated the day at Karekare, about seven kilometres away on the wild West Coast. They actually set out to walk over the hills of the Waitakeres to Piha and sat for a welcomed break on the cliff top looking down into the waters of Mercer Bay. They were soon revived by the rugged beauty and majesty of the barren hills, the seclusion and security of the bushclad ridges and hills about them. They were enchanted to watch the relentless waves from the Tasman Sea as strong prevailing westerly winds lifted them high before hurling them on to the foreshore's black sand. This caused white spray and foam to become strikingly outlined against the background of jagged rocks and boulders, which stoically endured the constant lashings by the cruel sea.

But the weather was not kind to them as it had been a year earlier. A storm quickly blew up, catching them by surprise while they were still a few kilometres from Piha. With no coats, they were caught in the midst of it. Hurrying back to Karekare and the old boarding house with its iron stove, they found that a cliff face they had only minutes before comfortably traversed, was now a waterfall. As they waded through it, one of Kathleen's shoes collapsed. Under a great spreading karaka tree they tied it with flax and then continued their journey, sliding down the steep track to the shelter of Karekare Bay.

Kathleen's attire was now in sharp contrast to that which she had been clothed in twelve months earlier! But despite the handicaps of being caught unprepared in the midst of a local storm miles away from the comforts of home and civilisation, this experience ensured they would remember the day for ever.

Soon after, Edward's chicken farm in Acton, Worcestershire, failed and Blaiklock's parents returned to New Zealand. Both Blaiklock and Kathleen loathed owing money to anyone, including their parents and they worked hard in the early years of married life to pay back the money they had borrowed from Edward and Florence when they had bought the house. This they did in three years. A mortgage-free home, so early in their life together, formed a sound basis for financial stability all their days.

In June 1930, Paterson told Blaiklock he planned to take sabbatical leave the next year to visit South Africa, Oxford and Europe. He recommended to the University Council that a former associate of Blaiklock's from his Auckland Grammar School days, Ronald Mason, be appointed during his leave to help with junior Latin classes. Mason had qualified for a Latin scholarship and Blaiklock was delighted.

Because of its shortage of funds, however, the Council refused the appointment. Paterson felt he had no alternative but to forego his leave. Realising how much Paterson was looking forward to it, Blaiklock offered to undertake the extra work that would fall to him with Paterson away. Paterson was amazed. 'If you could do that, it would indeed be a feather in your mortar-board,' he said.

Even though it would mean having to do more than double his number of lectures a week, with nine months preparation ahead of him, Blaiklock felt he could cope. Also, it would prove conclusively he had the ability to run the department without standards being sacrificed.

The year of Paterson's leave became a very full one for Blaiklock. As acting head of department, he put every ounce of energy and concentration he could muster into his work. He was rewarded at the end of it when the department won the Greek and Latin scholarships competed for by students from the University Colleges of New Zealand. On his return, Paterson was delighted.

On 31 March 1931, Blaiklock and Kathleen's first child, Peter, was born. Blaiklock was in his twenty-eighth year. Kathleen was delighted at becoming a mother. She had had labour pains for twenty-four hours and her groanings had been heard by Blaiklock – the maternity home was next door to their own home.

A close friend from school days, Janet Hesse, was the first to call at the maternity home. After visiting Kathleen and

## LECTURING AND MARRIAGE

seeing the new-born baby, Janet called next door to congratulate the father and found him quite upset. 'She's only next door and the Matron won't let me see her except during strict visiting hours,' he complained. After visiting Kathleen and holding his son in his arms, Blaiklock calmed down. But throughout Kathleen's confinement, the matron insisted Blaiklock kept strictly to visiting hours.

The year was an extremely full one for Blaiklock at the university. He also continued the lectures in Greek he was now doing at the Bible Training Institute established at the top of Queen Street by Rev Joseph Kemp. As well as all this, he was able to fit in some of his own studies and family responsibilities were not neglected.

In their early years of married life, Blaiklock and Kathleen adopted the traditional roles for husbands and wives – she did the flower garden and he the vegetable garden. Blaiklock liked to think their home was like that of Philemon and Baucis, of whom Ovid wrote:

> Ask not who in that home master was or maid
> They ruled together so that none could know.

Five kilometres from the Weston Avenue home, at Plunket Road, Mt Eden, lived Edward and Florence, now resigned to spending their remaining days in their adopted country. The time had finally passed for them when the lure of 'home' would again entice them to sell up and return to England.

About the same distance in the other direction from Weston Avenue, Kathleen's parents lived in their comfortable home on the high point of Blockhouse Bay where the 'blockhouse' (the soldiers' lookout post) had been manned day and night in the previous century during the land wars.

On occasions, the family would spend the day at Plunket Road, either walking the distance or travelling by the Owairaka tram. To Kathleen's parents at Blockhouse Bay, they walked there and back when they could fit in the time. They attended the Baptist Tabernacle services regularly and enjoyed the fellowship of its members. To Blaiklock and Kathleen, it seemed that life itself was smiling on them. It was certainly carrying them through calm and peaceful waters.

With the return of Paterson, 1932 was not nearly as heavy a year for Blaiklock as 1931 had been. But at the end of it, both Blaiklock and Kathleen decided they needed a good holiday. They accepted an invitation to stay with friends on their sheep farm in Southland for the month of January, 1933.

The mortgage was now paid up on the Weston Avenue home. Blaiklock felt he had already prepared reasonably thoroughly for the year ahead and the appeal of such a holiday for both was irresistible. Paterson had promised him overseas study leave in 1935 and he planned to continue in Britain the work he had already begun on a project on Lucretius. There would probably not be another opportunity between then and now for a holiday:

> We drank deep of the quiet rich life of the sheep hills. Precariously on horseback I helped to muster on our friends' farm in the Waikaka Valley. We bathed in the clean pools of the Pomahaka River and heard the bellbirds chiming with the tuis along the wild surf beaches below the low hills where the Catlins and Owaka streams joined to form the world's ultimate ocean. We read the history of 600 years where the tides had exposed the strata of a moa hunters' camp on the foreshore at Pounawea and where the first Polynesians, like other breeds of men, used up so prodigiously, the wealth which fed them. We watched from hiding the great king penguins ride the lurching waves and come cleverly to landing over the writhing cables of the sinister giant kelp. A month it was, of sequestered happiness.
>
> (*Between the Foothills and the Ridge*, p. 11)

There was no foreshadowing or even inkling of the dramatic events which lay just ahead.

While on holiday in Southland, Blaiklock received a letter from Paterson, saying he was taking a trip to Milford Sound on the Wanganella and would be away until into February. He had some matters about the new term he wanted to talk over and suggested they get together on his return before the start of the 1933 university year.

Relaxed and refreshed after their holiday, Blaiklock and Kathleen found the grass on their lawn was long and lush after more than the usual rain for a January. This was soon taken care of and Blaiklock then turned, with a sense of well-being, to revising his already prepared lecture programme for the months ahead. He expected the year to be a normal one and he was optimistically beginning to think of 1935 and his opportunity to study overseas, as promised by Paterson.

Even the worldwide recession seemed as if it might have peaked. Its effects were still being seriously felt in New Zealand but with prices overseas for bales of wool and carcasses of frozen meat on the increase, there was hope of better times ahead. And as yet, only a shadow of a cloud appeared on the world horizon from the rise of a young German politician called Hitler. Blaiklock saw Chesterton's verse about Baldur the Beautiful, fitting their circumstances perfectly at this time:

> There is always a thing forgotten
> When all the world goes well . . .

Paterson arrived back in the city a week after Blaiklock. There was no time for them to get together. He had to undergo a minor operation and after a few days in hospital, he wrote, he would be in touch with him again. The operation turned out to be far from minor. Paterson collapsed during it and forty-eight hours later died from septicaemia. It was 13 February 1933. Paterson was fifty-eight years old.

On Paterson's headstone at Purewa Lawn Cemetery, Blaiklock wrote, *Non omnis obiit* – 'he is not at all dead'. 'The gifts he gave me are still part of me', Blaiklock wrote forty-eight years later (*Between the Foothills and the Ridge*, p. 14). Paterson had influenced Blaiklock's university career more than any other single person. He had taught him the meaning of scholarship, to watch particularly the commonly forgotten links between classical and semitic studies and also to understand the unity of ancient history.

Paterson was one of the most learned teachers the Dominion has ever possessed and represented all that was best in the truest culture. He was much beloved, having a most delightful and winsome personality which gained him a wide circle of friends, not least among the students themselves.
(University Council minutes, 20 February 1933)

Professor Paterson's regime was undoubtedly a Golden Age in the Department's history. The Department had by 1933 attained to standards in both Greek and Latin instruction which were eminently worthy of the firm foundations laid by Professor Tucker. It had fallen to Professor Paterson's lot to gather together and set the seal on the work done by his predecessors and he had performed this task with outstanding success. Classics in Auckland was flourishing . . .
(W F Richardson and L W A Crawley, *Classics in Auckland*, p. 48)

There was no doubt Professor Paterson had considered Blaiklock one who could possibly succeed him in future years when his retirement came. At its meeting on 19 November 1932, less than three months before the Professor died, the University Council had received a request from him that Blaiklock should be appointed associate professor:

. . . if it is Council's wish that a full course of work in Greek should continue to be made available to students, steps should at once be taken to appoint a fulltime lecturer in Greek. Only by such an appointment can efficiency be secured without imposing an undue burden upon the present staff.

In the event of such an appointment proving impossible, in view of the present financial stringency, I have another suggestion to make. I have an exceedingly able and hardworking assistant in the person of Mr E M Blaiklock. I have on several occasions spoken of his work in the highest terms, more particularly in the report which I submitted to Council shortly after my return from leave.

As I am a professor and draw a professor's salary, while Mr Blaiklock is a lecturer on a lecturer's salary, I have hitherto felt it only fair that in the apportionment of the work I should take slightly the larger half. Thus Mr Blaiklock has this year 12 hours of lecturing per week as against my 15.

I do not wish Council to be under any misapprehension; Mr Blaiklock has, in my opinion, earned every penny of his salary and something over, but he is a young man who requires time of his own for further study and I have never until now entertained any idea of lightening my load at his expense. At the same time . . . some relief I must have and recent happenings have suggested a method. During my year of absence (1931) Mr Blaiklock did admirable work as Acting Professor and if he were now made Associate Professor, with the additional emolument attaching to such a post, I should have no compunction in adding three or four hours to his weekly total . . .

The University Council had voted to hold a special meeting over the question and on 3 November Professor Paterson had been interviewed. 'After a full discussion it was resolved to leave the matter in the hands of a committee, consisting of the President, Vice-President, Dr Ranston and Mr Mahon, with power to act' (University Council minutes 3 November 1932). But the Council had no opportunity to interview Paterson before he died – just seven days before the next Council meeting on 20 February 1933.

A few months later, in July 1933, Rev Joseph Kemp of the Bible Training Institute died from a brain tumour. It was unusual that Blaiklock should, in just a few months, be deprived of two mentors who had so profoundly influenced his life. But their work with Blaiklock, in one sense, had been completed. By that time he was firmly on the road to a potentially brilliant university career. Professor Paterson's request to the University Council in 1932 that he be made associate professor was testimony enough to Blaiklock's academic competence and maturity.

By that time also, theologically speaking, Blaiklock had become what he called 'an informed conservative'. His studies in the language and literature of the centuries of history in which the Bible was born were occasions where his honest zeal for truth and objective interpretation were never more severally tested. He had examined thoroughly the three main categories into which Christians in those years described themselves theologically.

Modernism was 'the humanistic tendency in religious

thought to supplement old theological creeds and dogmas by new scientific and philosophical learning and thus to place emphasis on practical ethics and worldwide social justice'. He rejected it as 'an arid and moribund radicalism by which many were finding their way out of the Church into agnosticism' (*The Bible and I*, p. 24).

Liberalism was 'in Protestant church bodies, an attitude favouring the use of methods of historical criticism on the Bible, wide leeway for individual interpretation of creeds, doctrines and ritual, and latitude as to methods of church government and congregational organisation: opposed to fundamentalism'. Blaiklock wrote of his view of it as follows: 'It is a pity that in so many spheres of thought the word "liberal" and its cognates have arrogantly assumed meanings which are far from what a pure concept of liberty should mean' (*The Bible and I*, p. 24).

Fundamentalism was 'the belief that all statements in the Bible are literally true'. Of fundamentalism, Blaiklock wrote that it 'contained all and much more of those oddities of interpretation and exegesis than I could accept. The separation, polemical and passionately controversial approach which so often accompanied such profession, also alienated me' (*The Bible and I*, p. 24).

So, if he were to wear a theological label (he never found it easy to fit completely into any of man's denominational or theological classifications), it was as an 'informed conservative'. This involved for Blaiklock, as he wrote in his retirement years,

> a jealous conservation of an authoritative Bible (without the loftiest doctrine of inspiration, that which Scripture teaches cannot be advanced, preached or taught with cogency or confidence) . . . a divine Christ, an atoning death, a unified Bible with a nation's history and a unified New Testament with no dichotomy between Christ and Paul.
>
> Once shake substantially the authority of Scripture and the haphazard collection of documents into which the Bible dissolves, becomes a happy hunting ground for theorists. Interpretation, devout or clever, becomes rationalist, subjective, secular. The Bible ceases to speak, if it is no longer the Word of God. Nor does it solve the dilemma to state that amid a welter

of human groupings, it merely contains the Word of God. Authority must be objective, not according to a reader's whim or fluctuating choice.

Informed conservatism welcomes all the light which learned research can throw on Scripture. It is no devotee of literalism, nor committed to Ussher's dates, a 'futurist' view of the Apocalypse, or to the text of the King James Version. Its view of Scripture can absorb all genuine discovery, although it has sometimes failed to demonstrate that confidence, and opposed where it should have adapted.

(*The Bible and I*, p. 28–29)

It was from the death of Professor Paterson that Blaiklock's career aspirations suffered most. He would have preferred a longer tutorship under the professor but he had proved to himself and to the University Council that he was competent to run the department. Had the committee set up by the Council to meet with the professor been able to do so before Paterson's sudden death, it seems certain it would have recommended the appointment of Blaiklock as an associate professor.

Immediately after Paterson's death, the chancellor of the university, Sir George Fowlds, called Blaiklock to his office. He was aware, he told him, that two years before Blaiklock had directed the department while Paterson had been on leave. Could he repeat the effort this year?

Blaiklock pointed out to Sir George that for his 1931 effort, he had had nine months to prepare. Now, in the middle of February, he had only a fortnight. Sir George promised that if Blaiklock repeated his 1931 effort, he could count on being appointed to the Chair of Classics to take Professor Paterson's place.

Apparently Sir George had promised chairs to two other lecturers also. The Council was not able to make good on any of the promises:

> . . . the two men always claimed, and Cocker and other Council members accepted this, that Sir George Fowlds had promised them Chairs when finances permitted. Similarly E M Blaiklock . . . was promised a Chair by Fowlds. He had no authority from Council to make any of these promises. In those

days there seems to have been a great deal of promising, notably by Fowlds and perhaps by O'Shea. Since no regular procedures had been established for appointments, hopes informally raised could sometimes be satisfied.
(Sir Keith Sinclair, *A History of the University of Auckland 1883–1983*, p. 192)

For Blaiklock, in his thirtieth year, the prize was a glittering one and the challenge, despite the herculean effort involved, was one he could not refuse. At its meeting on 20 February 1933 the Council appointed him acting head of the Department of Classics and, on 8 May, resolved to advertise the vacant Chair of Classics.

Apart from the pressures in the Classics Department following the death of Paterson, the year was not a happy one for the university as a whole and this added to the atmosphere of tension in which Blaiklock worked. There were rumblings about the leadership of the Biology and Chemistry Departments and questions about the performance of the registrar. Then in the winter of 1933 a full blown controversy arose over the question of academic freedom.

In 1932, a lecturer in philosophy with whom Blaiklock had formed a close friendship while both had been students at Training College, R P Anschutz, wrote a foreword to a book *A New Zealand Woman in Russia*, written by a communist, Mrs H J Scott.

Anschutz, who had put his address as the university on his foreword with his signature, was publicly rebuked for his views by the Minister of Education. The controversy spread far beyond the question of whether a staff member of the university should write in laudable terms of Soviet Russia. It included morality in general and was later regarded by some as signifying the birth of the permissive society in New Zealand. The issue had no major relevance for Blaiklock personally but it did affect him indirectly.

New elections to the University Council were held in April. Two of its members were to be appointed by the Court of Convocation (graduates and undergraduates). A newcomer to stand for election was W H Cocker, a lawyer and an academic who had studied at Cambridge, receiving first-class honours in law. He was also a strong advocate of academic freedom and at the Court of Convocation urged that there should be no interference to freedom of opinion and expression from either politicians or the University Council.

At the meeting of the Court of Convocation, a sitting member, Dr H Ranston, also spoke. He was New Zealand's first doctor of literature and principal of the Methodist Theological School, he had been a close personal friend of the late Professor Paterson and was also a friend of Blaiklock.

In his address to the Court of Convocation, Dr Ranston supported the chancellor's memorandum on academic freedom, the controversial aspects of which were the words 'in any public statement by a member of the College staff . . . the attitude should be a detached and impersonal one' and that such a responsibility was 'intimately related to the question of fitness for tenure of a University post'. This meant that a staff member virtually did not have freedom of expression. The Council alone would decide whether views expressed were 'detached and impersonal' and if it determined they were not, such a member could not be considered a fit person to hold a University post.

The meeting overwhelmingly voted for Cocker's viewpoint. Both speakers published brochures outlining their views. One of the signatories on Dr Ranston's pamphlet was Blaiklock, together with other lecturers and a number of professors. This was regarded as the conservative view in the academic freedom vote. Cocker was elected to the Council and Ranston defeated. In personal terms, it meant Blaiklock had lost another possible Council supporter. Having aligned himself with Ranston and against the new member and being politically conservative, Blaiklock was well aware he could not count on support from Cocker.

In those years New Zealand was still regarded very much as a colony of Great Britain. There were a few New Zealand professors but mostly the top positions went to overseas applicants. This was another factor counting against Blaiklock and about which he had spoken to Professor

Paterson when the latter had first suggested Blaiklock should join his department.

On the morning of their fifth wedding anniversary, 13 November 1933, Blaiklock and Kathleen opened the *New Zealand Herald* to read of the appointment to the Auckland University of four new professors. His name was not one of them. The Chair of Classics went to a Scotsman, Professor Charles Gordon Cooper, a few months younger in age than Blaiklock and a lecturer in Latin at the University of Liverpool. If there were any softening of the bitter pill Blaiklock now had to swallow, it was the knowledge that he was not the only senior lecturer to suffer similarly from 'overseas' being regarded as a superior qualification for applicants to senior university positions.

## 5   CAREER CRISIS

The implications for Blaiklock were shattering. So certain had he and Kathleen been that the path they were on was the right one; so secure had they felt with Professor Paterson at the university as Blaiklock's mentor and Joseph Kemp as their spiritual overseer. With both gone, life became dramatically different for them. The sudden change in circumstances seemed to Blaiklock too incredible to be real. It was as if he were living through a nightmare from which he would soon awake. Life, which had been smiling so sweetly on him since his marriage and his lectureship at the university, now engulfed him in billowing waves of despair and despondency.

It was not just that his hopes of attaining the Chair of Classics were dashed. Both opportunities to study overseas were now gone. In choosing Paterson's promise of two years' leave in the early 1930s, he had chosen what then had seemed the better option. He now had neither.

> Professor Cooper's preparation for a Chair in Classics had been slightly unusual. His successful career in the University of St Andrews had been followed by post graduate work on the Continent and in North Africa. He then abandoned Classics for journalism, working for British provincial papers for some years, before rejoining the academic world as Instructor in Classics in the University of Western Ontario. He was 26 years of age when he returned to the United Kingdom as lecturer in Latin at the University of Liverpool, the position he held immediately prior to his appointment to the Chair in Auckland.
> (*Classics in Auckland*, written by W F Richardson and L W A Crawley, published by the University of Auckland's classics Department, p. 60)

The position was obviously as important to Cooper as it was to Blaiklock and the former's tenure of office was unlikely to be short. There was no reason why, if he found life amenable in New Zealand, that Professor Cooper should not see out the remainder of his academic life in the chair.

One friend who understood something of the trauma the Blaiklocks were experiencing was Will Fortune, one of Blaiklock's older students, later to become a cabinet minister. He called at the Weston Avenue home early that morning and took them for a drive through the quietness and beauty of the Waitakere hills. Conversation during the more than hour-long journey was minimal. It was not the time for words and Kathleen, in her own quiet way, equally shared her husband's disappointment and understood his deep despair.

There was nothing Will Fortune could say to soften the blow. But his action that day meant more than thousands of words of sympathy. For someone to express one's understanding in so practical and unpretentious a manner was a soothing antidote to their anguish and inner turmoil.

When faced with difficult decisions previously, Blaiklock had turned to Paterson and/or Kemp. Now he turned to a man with whom he had established a close friendship through his lecturing at the Bible Training Institute.

The chairman of the Bible Training Institute, Robert A Laidlaw, was the founder-director of the Farmers Trading Company Ltd, a major New Zealand departmental store. Laidlaw was a young man and also a Christian when he had started his business in Dunedin years before. At that time he had made a 'pact with God' to contribute regularly to Christian work from the profits of the company. He had moved his business to Auckland in the 1920s and had continued being faithful to his 'pact'. At this time about fifty percent of profits from the business were being paid into a Christian trust.

It was not funds Blaiklock was in need of but counselling regarding his future. On a number of occasions he talked at length with Laidlaw in the latter's company office in Hobson Street, a short walk from the university. A long-time believer that the Bible could mean little or nothing unless one was prepared to translate its precepts into daily experience, Laidlaw challenged Blaiklock to face his present circumstances in the light of scripture. He emphasised particularly the passage where the apostle Paul claimed that for the Christian, who in faith laid hold of the totality of life and caught its meaning, 'all things worked together for good'. There was no circumstance in life, however bitter or seemingly unjust, Laidlaw explained, that was incapable of transformation.

For an older man already at the height of success, this might be easy to accept and recommend, Blaiklock rationalised. But for him, frustrated, disappointed and unjustly treated, it seemed impossible. How this injustice could in any way be 'transformed' as Laidlaw suggested, he could not see. His faith at that time did not stretch to his accepting that good could come from his circumstances.

Blaiklock searched for alternatives to continuing at the university. He was informed of a vacancy for a teacher of Greek in one of England's leading theological colleges and both he and Kathleen agreed to pursue the opportunity. But by the time they had come to this decision, the door of opportunity had closed.

Still hurt by his treatment at the university, and as a reaction to it, Blaiklock then applied for a position of headmaster of a New Zealand secondary school. He was not enthusiastic about his application, and when advised another person had been appointed was relieved. Finally, he decided the only course open to him was to remain where he was:

> I played with the notion of going to Cambridge and starting all over again, with due attention to a 'piece of paper' about Greek. Not Oxford now, whose degree I thought too philosophy-ridden. As for Lucretius, I had put the Oxford text by Cyril Bailey, with its interleaved notes, back on the shelf.
> (*Between the Foothills and the Ridge*, p. 20)

Sir George Fowlds invited Blaiklock to tea and dissuaded him from seeking another position. Political uncertainties in Europe also helped to confirm for Blaiklock the decision he had made.

It was not easy for Professor Cooper, a young man of twenty-nine years, to follow in the steps of the older Professor Paterson. Both Paterson and before him Professor Dettman had been fatherly figures and Paterson had performed his task with outstanding success. Cooper also had to face Blaiklock's strong opposition and resentment that he had been given the job which Blaiklock considered rightly should have been his.

Professor Cooper was one of four new professors from overseas to be appointed at Auckland University that year ('the Year of the Four Professors'). All were determined to improve conditions in their departments and to raise standards. Cooper obviously did not want to be outdone by his colleagues in these respects. Also, it was inevitable that each of the new professors would have something of a 'colonialist' attitude towards New Zealanders.

In his centennial year *History of the University of Auckland* (p. 173–174), Sir Keith Sinclair wrote: 'Cooper arrived like a small, frenzied, new broom. He turned out to be punctilious, prickly, humourless and lacking in common sense.' The new professor took no steps to outline Blaiklock's work for him for the year ahead. In the 1933–34 summer vacation, then, Blaiklock could do no preparation for the year's lectures which he had always been accustomed to do so thoroughly in previous years. But as March approached, Blaiklock had no fears about lecturing without thoroughly prepared notes; he had been an avid reader of all the relevant books in his subjects. He didn't like first indications, however, of how the year might work out under the new regime.

When it began, Professor Cooper swept aside many of the methods Blaiklock had found to be successful. His system of tutorials, for example, in which he had students read their essays to him before discussing them together, was termed 'useless'. He informed Blaiklock also, that his responsibility in the department would be confined solely to his lecturing and he was forbidden to undertake personal counselling of students.

In comparison with the more than twenty lectures a week (plus administrative responsibilities) which Blaiklock had undertaken when Professor Paterson had been on leave, the new head of department decreed that four lectures a week were all that anyone should expect. At the start of the year Blaiklock lectured only two days a week. This was later increased to three, leaving his Wednesdays and Fridays completely free.

There was no doubt Blaiklock resented missing out on the job of professor. But there were other factors which entered into the fourteen-year personality clash between the two men.

Blaiklock could not have found it easy, after six years under Professor Paterson, adjusting to Cooper. He considered Cooper's scholarship in no way matched that of Paterson's and that Cooper's abilities were no greater than his own. Blaiklock too, was convinced he knew New Zealand students and how to develop their potential better than did Cooper. Another area of possible conflict for Blaiklock was journalism. Blaiklock had just started writing for the *New Zealand Herald* and with Cooper's several years full-time experience on British provincial newspapers, Blaiklock could well have felt threatened in this area also.

Furthermore, there were differences in temperament and social habits. Cooper was a keen sportsman – Blaiklock was not. A golfer, Cooper had the unusual habit of sometimes coming to university in plus fours. This, no doubt riled Blaiklock as it did other members of the staff. (Cooper might even have been Auckland University's first and only staff member to lecture in plus fours.)

Like many other Englishmen of that period, Cooper had difficulty understanding the 'colonial'. Where Paterson had recognised Blaiklock's potential and sought to encourage him, Cooper did the opposite. And did the edict that Blaiklock should not counsel students, stem from Cooper's disapproval of Blaiklock's puritannical zeal?

The principal of the Bible Training Institute and close friend of the Blaiklocks, J Oswald Sanders, commented on those years, 'Some of Blaiklock's actions and re-actions at that time could hardly be termed Christian,' but he did not elaborate. However, it was obvious that Blaiklock let his differences with Cooper be known to students and staff and also spoke about them to close friends. Cooper, for his part, seems to have been more reserved about sharing them with others.

Elizabeth Roberton was a student and then part-time lecturer in the Classics Department from 1934 to 1941. Referring to Professor Cooper, she says:

> This new, strange professor at first intimidated us. But I came to appreciate his ability. He was a first-class scholar and I became his honorary assistant in 1939.
>
> But he never really understood New Zealanders. With brilliant students such as the Rhodes Scholars, Speight and Cawkwell, he got on well. They had excellent brains and he was used to dealing with such minds. For the rest of us, so long as we had spent hours on our Latin proses, he didn't think of us as colonials.

At the beginning of 1939, Blaiklock became ill, suffering from duodenal ulcers. The tremendous workload he had carried in earlier years when acting head of the department, plus the strain with Professor Cooper, no doubt contributed to this. He was forced to take six weeks' leave from the university.

That year Elizabeth Roberton was taking Latin and Greek honours. Cooper took Blaiklock's lectures during Blaiklock's absence. On his return to the Greek honours class (about ten students) in the small lecture room opposite the professor's door, Blaiklock said: 'What His Majesty has spent doing in one term while I have been away, I will now do properly.' Blaiklock often referred in those years to Cooper as 'His Majesty' and there was never any doubt with students to whom he was referring. Elizabeth was incensed at this slight to Professor Cooper and picking up her books, walked out of the lecture room. On several occasions following this incident, Blaiklock asked her to return but each time she refused. She kept in touch with other students in the class and returned to the group only when Blaiklock had finished going over the same work Professor Cooper had already done.

Elizabeth was generally on good terms with both lecturers. She knew Professor Cooper well and on a number of occasions, with other students, was invited to his home. At no time did she hear Professor Cooper speak disparagingly of Blaiklock. However, Cooper was, she said, a man of moods and not the easiest to get on with.

So concerned did the University Council become over the differences between Cooper and Blaiklock, that in 1938 they decided to separate the teaching of Greek from the control of the professor and make Blaiklock responsible for it. Cooper remained directly responsible to the Council for Latin and Blaiklock for Greek.

With a full Greek school from first year to MA, averaging about fifty students, Blaiklock was now required to give a great deal more time to the university with tutorials as well as lectures. He loved the close encounter with young people, instructing them, catching the flash of his own enthusiasm on intelligent faces and knowing his endeavours were marked and appreciated. When locked into the Cooper regime, he had lost most of his enthusiasm and its rewarding joy in lecturing. Now he found it exhilarating to be back again.

'I was back', he wrote later, 'for teaching purposes to the more minute analysis of prescribed texts, to textual criticism, philology and syntax; whoever was directing my studies was giving me precisely what I needed . . .' (*Between the Foothills and the Ridge*, p. 37).

In 1941 the Council made official the separation of the Classics Department into two sections. At its meeting of 29 May the Council was informed that in discussions with the chairman of the Professorial Board, Professor Cooper had stated he considered the division academically unsound but that he was prepared to do everything possible to make it work.

The Council's executive committee had discussed the matter with Blaiklock who also had said that he was prepared to do everything he could to assist in the smooth working of the scheme. In the resolution making the division official, the following words were added: 'The adoption of the scheme for allocation of duties is not intended to imply any reflection upon either Professor Cooper or Mr Blaiklock in the carrying out of their duties in the

Department' (University Council minutes, 29 May, 1941).

In his report to the June meeting of the Council, Cooper's pettiness and animosity to Blaiklock surfaced. He had previously received Blaiklock's report (for the Council) on the latter's work in Greek and Cooper had included it with his own. Blaiklock headed his report 'Greek Department', and pointed out that one of his Greek students had won the senior scholarship. Cooper questioned this, saying the student had only shared the scholarship with a Wellington student with whom she had been placed equal first.

And he couldn't let pass Blaiklock's reference to a 'Greek Department'. It was, Cooper suggested, obviously a *lapsus calami* (slip of the pen).

With his greatly reduced responsibility in the Classics Department, beginning from 1934, Blaiklock had had an invaluable opportunity to pursue his own studies. He had continued reading more widely than ever before, learning German and Italian and working through classics books from the library in these languages. For this he had used the Paterson Collection, 'for that fine private library (of Professor Paterson) had been willed to the University'.

His favourite study was Greek and during 1934 he had read the five massive volumes of the *Expositor's Greek Testament*. These volumes had been a present from Rev Joseph Kemp in return for Blaiklock occupying the Baptist Tabernacle pulpit in 1932 while Kemp had been on leave. Blaiklock had also, in 1934–35, dug deeply into Vergil, reading everything about him he could find in the general and the periodical literature. It was during this period that Blaiklock discovered Arnold Toynbee's *Study of History*, which he reviewed for the *New Zealand Herald*.

An English historian best known for his comparative studies of civilisations, Toynbee was Professor of Byzantine and Modern Greek Language, Literature and History at the University of London from 1919 to 1924. His major work was his *Study of History*, published in ten volumes.

Toynbee's thesis was that it is not nations or periods that are significant units of historical study but societies or civilisations. Toynbee's critics have insisted, however, that no comparison among civilisations is possible, each being a unique ensemble with no relevant similarity to one another.

Blaiklock became captivated by Toynbee and his theories of history:

> I read Toynbee in those years on the collapse of cultures . . . Worlds end, as T S Eliot saw, 'with a whimper', not an explosion. The jungle is always waiting, as Lucretius said, 'with mighty maw agape'. When life seems cabined there must be no giving up. The road runs on, if need be into the Red Sea. Works broken must be set up again. Coolness must meet the hostile spears closing in. We were striving to live out those resolves as the 1930's sped.
> (*Between the Foothills and the Ridge*, p. 33)

Another subject which Blaiklock became increasingly fascinated by was archaeology. It was making spectacular advances in these years and Blaiklock undertook a rapid reading course to keep himself up-to-date with it.

In archaeology and particularly ancient history, he found many lessons applicable to life in the twentieth century, and sought to make this knowledge available to others outside university circles wherever possible. He welcomed, therefore, the opportunity that presented itself at this time for a writing career that was to last over 40 years and win him the reputation of becoming New Zealand's most widely read and best known newspaper columnist.

# 6  JOURNALISM AND A THESIS

In 1933, Blaiklock had decided to try his hand at journalism. The literary editor of the country's largest daily newspaper, the *New Zealand Herald* owned by Wilson and Horton, Dan Holland, was always on the lookout for competent reviewers of new books. Those on classical subjects he passed to the Classics Department at the university. Blaiklock had decided to review one himself and had taken his effort to the newspaper office where he met Dan Holland. He had been surprised and pleased to learn that Holland also lived on the slopes of Mt Albert – he the western slopes, Blaiklock the southern.

Holland's daughter, Joan Holland (now principal of St Cuthbert's Girls School in Epsom, Auckland), clearly remembers her father's friendship with Blaiklock: 'As a young girl I often had to deliver books or newspaper articles to the Blaiklock home,' she says. 'Dad always used to boast that he had taught Blaiklock how to write for a newspaper.'

As well as book reviews, Blaiklock was also asked to write editorials for the paper's leader page. In charge of this section of the paper was OS (Budge) Hintz (he became editor from 1958 to 1970). Blaiklock's editorials covered a wide variety of subjects and appeared on Saturdays. Hintz was impressed with Blaiklock's style and always studied his contributions before sending them on to the printer. 'Much of what he wrote influenced my own writing,' Hintz said.

In 1934 Kathleen became pregnant again. But hopes of another child were dashed when she miscarried. In October the next year, however, their second son David was born. Both now agreed two children were enough.

The same year Kathleen suffered the loss of her brother Cliff, killed while a missionary of the Sudan Interior

Mission in Abyssinia. He was speared to death by natives in revolt against the invasion of their country by the Italian dictator, Mussolini.

Before he had gone overseas in 1931, Cliff had visited Kathleen to say goodbye. At the time, Kathleen had had a strange foreboding as she had watched him leave the Weston Avenue home to catch the Avondale tram and eventually the ship. Kathleen's friend Janet Hesse had also been present at the time. 'Kathleen was very apprehensive about Cliff at that time,' she says. Forgetting for the moment that Janet was there, Kathleen mused to herself in words loud enough for Janet to hear: 'I wonder if I shall ever see him again.'

Soon after his arrival in Africa, Cliff married Myrtle Jenkins, a New Zealander from Underwood, Invercargill, and also a missionary with the same society. They were put in charge of a pioneer station at Darassa, in the Sidamo Province of Southern Abyssinia.

Armed forces of the Italian dictator Mussolini invaded the country in 1935 and in October of that year, Cliff, aged thirty-four, and Myrtle, were ordered by the governor of the province to move from Darassa to Yerga Alem, the province's capital.

Following the threat by the Italians in the south, Cliff took Myrtle and their young son to Addis Ababa, the capital of the country, to ensure their safety. Being satisfied with security there, Cliff returned to Sidamo to continue missionary work and also to help the Red Cross.

On 7 May 1936, Cliff and Thomas Devers, a Canadian missionary with whom he was working, heard by radio that the Italian army was advancing on Addis Ababa. The latter's fiancee was also in the capital. Becoming exceedingly concerned about the safety of the women, both men decided to make their way back to the capital by the shortest route possible.

They had no knowledge that a major riot had already taken place in the capital following the flight of Emperor Haile Selassie; nor that they would almost certainly meet large numbers of angry, warlike local tribesmen on the route they had chosen. However, they gathered together a party of twenty-five friendly tribesmen to travel with them in case of difficulties. But the number was insufficient. At about 2 p.m. on 9 May the party was attacked by about 200 Arussi Gallas armed with rifles and spears.

It was not until the end of August that Myrtle, still waiting anxiously in Addis Ababa for news, received official word from the British Legation in the capital that Cliff and Tom had been speared to death. The legation had been informed by another New Zealand missionary who had been in the province at another station at the time. In July, when the situation in the province deteriorated still further, he had moved south to the Kenyan border for his safety.

He had talked with one of the missionaries' original twenty-five helpers who had escaped the massacre. The news he gave was that both missionaries had been speared to death about the same time. Many of the friendly tribesmen accompanying them had also been killed and their bodies left on the road. The assaulting tribesmen must have been concerned, however, when they discovered they had killed two white missionaries, for they had dragged their bodies under nearby bushes. That was the last information ever received about the pair. Their bodies were never recovered.

After three months of uncertainty over Cliff's whereabouts, news of his death came as a shock to Kathleen and Blaiklock. With the African country still occupied by the Italians, there was nothing they could do about it from New Zealand, and this made their grieving harder to bear.

Next to where Blaiklock and Cliff in their youth had so often struck camp at Wood Bay, a plum tree had sprung up. This they had agreed could have come only from one of the many plum stones they had thrown out of their tent during their camping periods. After Cliff's death, the tree became a silent memorial to Cliff and to the times Blaiklock and he had spent together on the Manukau. Blaiklock and Kathleen could never again walk along that shore without the tree recalling the tragedy vividly to them. As much as possible, they avoided it.

When the Italians were finally driven out of Abyssinia by British forces in 1941, Blaiklock wrote to General Cunningham, in charge of the British East African Force Headquarters in Nairobi, Kenya, seeking any information the Army might have received about Cliff Mitchell. In 1941 he received a reply from Lieutenant-Colonel W D Dickinson, General Staff Intelligence at Nairobi, to whom Blaiklock's letter had been referred:

> ... I have but recently returned from Abyssinia and passed through the Darassa country where I made the fullest inquiries and endeavoured to find out anything about your brother-in-law. I regret to say I was unsuccessful. Even his old house had been thoroughly looted and destroyed by the Abyssinians – an art at which they are particularly adept. So after waiting many months for news, I am unable to give you any ...

Blaiklock himself had been too young to be a participant in the First World War and, because of duodenal ulcers, was denied an active role in the Second on the grounds of his health. But he did what he could for the war effort, lecturing one night a week at the Officers' Training School at Narrow Neck, for nearly three years. He dealt with the history of warfare, tactics, and the causes and nature of human conflict. He also addressed interested groups and societies on public affairs and when a Japanese invasion seemed imminent, spent one evening a week with suburban groups mobilised for civil defence.

In 1941 the *Weekly News* editor, H I Macpherson, asked Blaiklock to write a regular column 'on whatever a classical scholar may have in mind'. His first contribution, entitled 'Re-thinking History', was on archaeology and published under his own name, on 16 February 1941. The significance he placed on the subject and its findings, is seen in the introductory paragraphs of his article:

> The world of the ancients was a wider place than modern men have imagined. When Europe woke from the Dark Ages and a passion for things new sent the navigators east and west, the brightness of the new dawn made men forget that it had once been day before. It was centuries before men found that the Northmen had visited the New World long before Columbus. The story how Phoenician voyagers anticipated Vasco da

Gama by sailing round the Cape 2000 years before the Portuguese was a distrusted chapter in Herodotus.

The archaeologists have sobered modern pride. Chinese pottery has been found in Rhodesia. Traces of the Greeks extend into China. Undoubted products of Sumeria have been recovered from the silt which covers the ancient culture of the Indus Valley. Swedish peat-bogs hide exports from Rome. India is full of Greek and Roman coins. When such a wealth of evidence survives the ruin of the centuries, it is easy to see how incorrect was the notion that confined the ancient world to the Inland Sea, hemmed in by the barbarians.

Blaiklock was then asked to write a regular weekly article for the *Weekly News*, using a pen name: 'At first I was apprehensive about whether I could continue indefinitely but soon after the appointment, I chanced to be alone in the house for a whole week and writing hard, stored up some two dozen articles. That gave me confidence' (*Between the Foothills and the Ridge*, p. 63–64).

Grammaticus articles began with the first issue of 1942. Blaiklock chose his pen name because it meant 'a teacher of literature and language the nearest equivalent in ancient Rome to a university professor in such a discipline today'. Grammaticus articles continued in Wilson and Horton's different publications – the *Weekly News*, and when that died, the *Sunday Herald*, and when that suffered a similar fate, the *New Zealand Herald* – without missing a week for over forty-one years.

Blaiklock was also preaching regularly in Baptist churches in and around Auckland and in 1944, became a member of the Baptist Theological Board, succeeding in getting the board to agree to first-year students taking Greek at Auckland University. The principal of the Baptist College, Dr J J North, was never enthusiastic about the idea. It was more important, he said, that students should become theologians than Grecians. But he agreed to the idea nevertheless.

One of two new students that year who became the 'guinea pigs' for the short-lived experiment, was Bob Thompson. The workload for the two young students became excessive. Thompson survived, but his companion, after only one term, didn't. Thompson continued at university as he completed his theological training.

Blaiklock was sometimes criticised for using uncommon words difficult for his hearers to understand. Thompson recalls a judge in a court hearing in 1943 delaying the case so he could consult a dictionary over the word 'cacophonous' which Blaiklock had used in giving evidence for Dr North.

It was a case in which the Baptist College principal had been sued for libel as a result of an article he wrote about an adventist group and their prophecy on the second coming of Christ. The return of Christ was to take place on 17 July 1944, the group had predicted. Their calculations, expressed in verse, had been based on the number of words in the English Bible, not the Greek Testament. Dr North had called them 'impudent prophets'. He called Blaiklock to testify that the Greek total was quite different from the English. The libel did not succeed, 17 July 1944 came and went and the 'prophets' were not heard of again.

According to Thompson, Blaiklock was always impatient with the liberal element in the Baptist denomination. Successor to Dr North, Rev Luke Jenkins, was of that tradition. Blaiklock opposed his appointment, ultimately resigning from the Baptist Theological Board in protest.

With his own Greek 'department', writing and Christian activities, Blaiklock continued to live a full life. For relaxation, the family continued to travel, usually once a week, to Titirangi amid the peaceful surroundings of the Waitakeres, with which they were so familiar:

> We took the train and walked from the New Lynn station to an empty Titirangi . . . I had retreated there before from stress and found my peace . . . Sitting at lunch on Mt Atkinson with both harbours at our feet, we felt removed from the University . . . We talked of life and love amid the understanding silence of its trees. I can never look without a gripping at heart, at the totara under which we would sometimes sit, a sapling then, which heard what we discussed and the strong conclusions reached – conclusions which need two to bring to final thought. It was a rich fellowship and we were under no

illusions that the wealth which had come into our lives meant more than could ever come by the whim of men, or the convulsions of an academic career. We would come home for tea and sunset in the window, refreshed in spirit; more closely one, if that were possible; more convinced that the future held much concealed and invigorated to do what lay in hand to do and to improve the shining hour which could not last forever.
(*Between the Foothills and the Ridge*, p. 28–29)

In the 1940s, Blaiklock's Greek section flourished and in the years 1940–46, four of his students became Rhodes Scholars. They were M W Speight (killed at Cassino in the Second World War), G L Cawkwell, B F Harris and F Foulkes. During these years Blaiklock concentrated particularly on his own studies in Greek, still worried that he had 'no piece of paper' in that language. He read all the thirty-five surviving tragedies in Greek, seeing their unity and evolution. This was excellent groundwork for his thesis *The Male Characters of Euripides*, which won him a Ph.D. in literature in September 1945 and was published as a book by the University Press seven years later. The thesis was 'a study in realism' and 'in memoriam to Alfred Croom Paterson'. His 'piece of paper in Greek', problem was now solved. The book was reviewed favourably in the *New Zealand Herald*.

> Dr Blaiklock takes the view that Euripides was primarily a realist and was writing of what he saw about him. His touch of modernity has made him popular. Athens, in which he lived, does not seem an unfamiliar place, nor his age remote from ours. The stress of war was doing its ancient work on the hearts and minds of many and many a problem which still afflicts mankind was already seeking solutions on that ancient stage.

Euripides (485–407 BC) was the youngest of the three great Attic tragedians. The characteristics of his plays are their human qualities (men are represented in them in everyday life), their poignant realism and the frequent use of divine intervention. Two of his most remarkable plays are *Bacchae*, and *Heracles*. Others interpret Euripides' purpose in writing the *Bacchae* as being to teach moderation, the need for self-control on the one hand and the danger on the other, of too strong repression of natural instincts. Blaiklock saw it as a study of religious psychology from real life, Dionysus and his followers being a fanatical religious group living in Euripides' day. *Heracles*, according to Blaiklock, shows that Euripides had studied the disease of epilepsy in depth. He used Heracles as the vehicle of his observations.

A month after being awarded his Ph.D., another major event for Blaiklock and family took place. Ever since their marriage, Blaiklock and Kathleen had lived in the same house. Now they made their one and only move of their home in their lives – to 47 Koromiko Road, Titirangi.

The plot had a special significance for Blaiklock as it overlooked the valley where he had spent his childhood and where his father had farmed unsuccessfully. Some of the trees his father had planted in those early days could be clearly identified from the new home. Situated on the northern slopes of the Waitakere Range, its wide-angled view covered the city with its two harbours, one on either side. It was eleven miles from Auckland University.

The family celebrated their first night there seated before a large lounge window silently watching the distant city become a mass of twinkling fairy-like lights below them. It all had an air of unreality for them but this was soon to become commonplace.

When they had lived at Weston Avenue, walks with the boys up Mt Albert were frequent. Now they enjoyed happy days of relaxation exploring together the Waitakere Range as far as Whatipu on the edge of the rugged West Coast shoreline. Its surf-pounding beaches appealed particularly to Blaiklock and these excursions did much to strengthen existing bonds between father and sons.

The Waitakeres had so many magnificent and unusual places to explore. It was four miles from Whatipu to Pararaha Point and then on to Gibbons track, the old lorry road from Karekare used in the timber milling days. One impressive sight was from the 600ft cliff about a mile south of Pararaha Point: they could watch whisps of smoke coming from the now ebbing fire they had lit on the beach the previous day, with the rolling surf as the backdrop to the long stretch of beach; then towards evening, they could see from their unique vantage point the spectacular sunsets so much a feature of that part of Auckland.

There were nights in the rough old Whatipu Fishing Lodge with only a kerosene lamp for light. Following a day's walk in the salt air in the hills, evening meals could be the choice of delicacies of wild pork and fish. On other occasions, they would cook a meal of sausages and boil their billy on a beach bonfire. To cap off the evenings, Blaiklock would then read from a novel he knew the boys would enjoy as much as he had done at their age and earlier: H Rider Haggard's *King Solomon's Mines*, or *She*.

At Huia, on the way to Whatipu, Blaiklock's friend from training college days and the church, Warnock Watson, had a holiday home. It was a convenient stopping-off place as they traversed the tracks past Bald Rock and Mt Donald McLean, through the Odlin Timber Company's bush roads of last century, down the valleys to the Pararaha Point, Karekare and along the Whatipu beach.

The two families often visited Whatipu together. Watson recalls that

> On one of the visits an unexpected tropical downpour turned part of the road up the hill to Huia into a quagmire. Blaiklock thought it a great joke as his son David, his legs pulled through the arms of a football jersey and the body stretched over his waist, became plastered with mud thrown up by the spinning back wheels as we tried to push the car out of a very sticky patch.

No home was complete without a family dog and the Blaiklocks had theirs – an Irish terrier they named Castlereagh Kerry. He took no time to settle down in his new surroundings. A friend and playmate for the boys, Kerry had cost four guineas, came with a pedigree and lived to the age of sixteen. Finally arthritis took over and his spine gave out. He had to be put down. When Blaiklock took him to his place of execution, it was as if Kerry, with his enquiring eyes and mournful, pleading look, knew the fate that awaited him at the hands of one in whom he had trusted for so many years! Blaiklock's sensitive nature rebelled at having to take such action but there was no other way of freeing Kerry from his old age frailties and the pain racking his little body.

Then there were lessons of life to be passed on to the boys in those years on the bushclad slopes of Titirangi during the 1940s and 50s. As well as in the community, the Blaiklocks sought to live as Christians before their sons. Differences between the parents there were, but rarely if ever did these blow up into arguments or antagonisms in which the security of the home was threatened. Kathleen's closest lifetime friend, Janet Hesse, says she knows of no occasion when Blaiklock and Kathleen had differences serious enough to threaten in any way, their relationship. Had there been any such occasion, Janet Hesse is convinced Kathleen would have confided in her.

Discipline was an area in which there was no lack of lessons from parents both by example and by word of mouth. David recalls when as a very young child, his father challenged him about his habit of thumb-sucking. 'Now David, you are the boss of your own body so you must stop sucking your thumb,' his father had exhorted him. David revered his father and feared him, especially when he sometimes became very angry. Blaiklock had no reason to remonstrate further with David concerning his childish habit. His method of dealing with it worked.

Another lesson Blaiklock sought to impress upon the boys was that faith and reason went together. 'Truth does not conflict with truth,' he would repeat often. Blaiklock deplored those who 'made Christianity impossible for ordinary people'. Christianity at times, he impressed upon them, went beyond one's full understanding but was never irrational.

Other lessons basic to the family upbringing included the boys being taught to be truthful under all circumstances and not to be afraid to stand up for what they believed in. Kathleen played her full part well into the teenage years of the boys and beyond. She was always supportive of Blaiklock, working from the background with him, helping to calm his spirit at times of tension or strife.

At the university, in the second half of the 1940s, the days were slowly moving to another crisis point for Blaiklock within the Classics Department. Professor Cooper was given sabbatical leave for 1947. This resulted in a unique situation developing during his absence. Each professor was automatically a member of the Professorial Board and when on leave, it was usually the senior lecturer who took his place. Before Professor Cooper went on leave, however, he left strict instructions that the Latin lecturer, Peter Crawley, was to represent him on the Professorial Board and not Blaiklock, who was senior lecturer.

To overcome a delicate situation, the Board appointed both Blaiklock and Crawley to represent the department, with the proviso that they would have only one vote between them. Fortunately there were no great differences of opinion between Blaiklock and Crawley, not personally and certainly not on key issues affecting the department. Thus the minutes secretary did not have to record half votes at Professorial Board meetings during Cooper's absence.

Professor Cooper never returned to Auckland University following his departure on sabbatical leave. He accepted the Chair of Classics at the University of Queensland.

> Cooper was unfortunate in arousing antagonism in many quarters where less insistence on rigid principles might have secured co-operation. The same characteristics, according to report, made his tenure of the Chair in Brisbane as uncomfortable as they had done in Auckland . . . He was a sincere scholar whose dogged loyalty to the standards he set was unfortunately not accompanied by the qualities to enlist recognition and appreciation.
> (*Classics in Auckland*, by W F Richardson and L W A Crawley, University of Auckland Classics Department, p. 77)

In December 1947, Blaiklock received a phone call from the president of Auckland University, W H Cocker, advising him of his appointment to the Chair of Classics. Blaiklock was the first New Zealander to be so appointed and the first member of the staff to be promoted to the Chair of Classics at the college for more than twenty years.

Cocker was the anti-establishment candidate of 1933 who became president in 1939 and, for a brief period in 1961, chancellor. He was leader of an inner circle which dominated the University Council for thirty years. In 1933 he had voted for the appointment of Professor Cooper to the Chair of Classics as against the promise Blaiklock had received from the then retired chairman, Sir George Fowlds.

In a newspaper interview in his retirement years, Blaiklock told of the hours he and Kathleen had spent together immediately preceding that telephone call for which they had been waiting fourteen years. They were walking together along Hongi's bush track in Rotorua when Blaiklock light-heartedly, threw the customary spring of fern under the Wishing Tree. He then made a petition, or wish in Latin, about 'the most difficult' problem he was facing. 'Kathleen challenged me to be serious', he told his newspaper interviewer. 'We drove down to Lake Rotoiti and committed the matter to God. As we reached home, the telephone was ringing. When I answered, a friend said he had good news for me. I knew what it was before he spoke – a 14-year problem had been lifted.'

While accepting that his failure to be appointed to the Chair of Classics in 1933 was the best thing that could have happened to him, Blaiklock could never forget the hurts of that time and the long years of conflict with Professor Cooper. In the early 1980s, in compiling his autobiography, he referred to those years but never once mentioned Professor Cooper (who died in Brisbane in 1973) by name:

> I met too much pain and care in the decade . . . I simply do not wish to write about it, much less to speak of those who caused it. It does not increase the stature of any man to write with frankness of those he could gladly not have met, especially when they themselves no longer tell their story.
> (*Between the Morning and the Afternoon*, p. 72)

# PART THREE:
# TWENTY-ONE YEARS IN THE CHAIR

# 7 LIVING LIFE TO THE FULL

With Blaiklock at last in the chair, the Classics Department in 1948 became integrated once again. Both Latin and Greek were now shared between the new professor and his senior lecturer, Peter Crawley, first appointed lecturer in Latin in 1938.

Crawley had been an honours student in Latin and Greek from both Auckland (1931) and Cambridge universities. He had served for nine years under Professor Cooper from whom he acknowledged he had received the utmost courtesy and consideration. Crawley had no complaints about the way Cooper shared out his work (*Classics in Auckland*, p. 67). He was thus familiar with the methods and characteristics of both Blaiklock and Cooper. In the long years of division between them, he had steered clear of taking sides. It was not difficult now for him to be working directly under Blaiklock. In fact, he welcomed the new era for the department with its release from the personality conflict which had so bedevilled it for so many years.

Blaiklock also welcomed the compatibility with Crawley and in his introduction to *Classics in Auckland*, written in his retirement and published in 1983, Blaiklock singled out Crawley for 'my special gratitude . . . His quiet friendship and firm participation in the Department's activities were a feature of the happiest 20 years of my University life.'

Blaiklock was pleased to be able to muster all his resources and abilities as he had done in 1931 and 1933 in running the department. Now in his middle forties, he was much more mature and content than he had been in his thirties.

Having achieved his ambition, he now accepted that the fourteen years under Cooper had enabled him to gain much that otherwise he would have been without. He realised he had been fortunate not to have been appointed to the chair in 1933.

The advantages for him had been many. His D.Litt. had given him some international recognition and he had a much firmer hold on the classics and classics on him. He was also well into semitic studies, another discipline he had taken up. His entry into journalism had given him the immensely satisfying task of leader writing for the *New Zealand Herald* and regular weekly Grammaticus articles for the *Auckland Weekly News*.

Despite his damaged health, the years had been full and rewarding ones for him in both his extra-mural activities and in his family life. His elevation to the chair now increased his status and his acceptance at home and abroad, particularly in his growing Christian ministries in churches and at seminars and conferences.

At the university, teaching was his delight and he kept Vergil for himself:

> Along with Cicero he formed the staple of our first-year syllabus. It was, I thought, important that those who stayed with us for one year only, should go on their way having made some acquaintance with one of the world's four or five greatest poets and with a master of commanding prose. I knew Vergil with some intimacy, sensed the pulse of his heart and mind and it was a joy to see one here, one there of those who listened, catch the vision and see the universal message in that great human being.
> (*Between the Foothills and the Ridge*, p. 51)

In classical education, Blaiklock went even further than Paterson, who, he was beginning to realise, might have overstressed the linguistic side.

> We sought to weld the linguistic training to the humanities. We held fast to the view that the documents in our hands were not collections of examples of alien grammar and syntax but of great literatures, the surviving records of two civilisations from which our own was descended. Their cultural value is priceless . . .
> (*Between the Foothills and the Ridge*, p. 50)

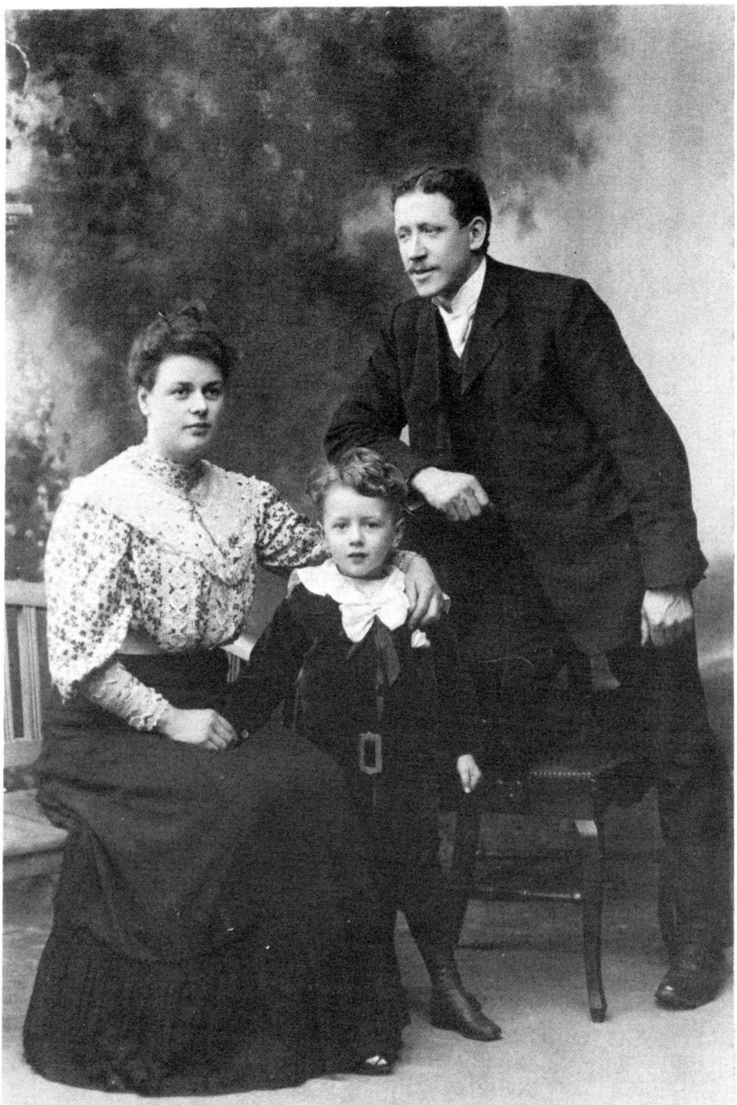

Drinkwater

DEANSGATE ARCADE
MANCHESTER
LONDON RD
LEICESTER
CORPORATION ST
BIRMINGHAM

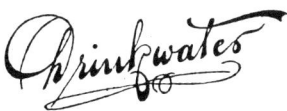

Edward (senior) and Florence Blaiklock shortly before emigrating to New Zealand from Birmingham in 1909, with their son Edward (junior).

16-year-old Edward Musgrave Blaiklock, as a pupil teacher in 1920.

*Top:* Kathleen, shortly before her marriage in 1928.

An informal wedding photo on the steps of the Auckland Baptist Tabernacle, 13 November, 1928. Cliff Mitchell, Kathleen's brother is in the foreground facing the camera.

Professor Blaiklock's parents, photographed in the early 1930s, after a return visit to England and having decided to live out their days in New Zealand.

Blaiklock and Cliff Mitchell's camping site at Wood Bay.

47 Koromiko Road, Titirangi, the Blaiklock home from 1945.

Blaiklock being congratulated by the President of the Auckland University, Mr W H Cocker, on being awarded a Doctorate in Literature for his thesis on the Male Characters of Euripides, September 1945.

Blaiklock in Queen Street, Auckland's main street, in February 1954.

*Above:* Taken outside Marshall and Snelgroves, Oxford Street, London, 1964.

*Centre:* During sabbatical leave in 1964, Blaiklock and Kathleen at the Afqa Spring, near the summit of a Lebanon range near Byblos.

*Below:* Blaiklock and Kathleen (left) at the second marriage of Blaiklock's University of Auckland friend and associate, Professor A C Keys. 26 August, 1965.

*Above left:* Blaiklock relaxes under two young kauri trees and the bush of his Titirangi home.

*Above right:* A few months before his death Blaiklock talks about one of his lifetime hobbies – collecting walking sticks.

The last photo taken of Professor Blaiklock one month before he died. He is shown with members of the Augustani group, from *left to right:* Hugh Cheeseman, Janice Cheeseman, Prof. Crawley, Dianne Ritchie, Mary Farrell (niece of Prof. Crawley), Bruce Baker, Karen Staniland, John Staniland, Vivienne Gray, Michael Farrell, Prof. Blaiklock. Absent Augustani members: Evan Gray, Michael Stevens.

Blaiklock took over a department with an already high scholastic standard to which he himself had contributed. Under him, the department maintained its academic standards and, coupled with the uninterrupted and harmonious association of the lecturers, had a long period of stable administration.

Blaiklock's father was glad to live long enough, and was also proud to see his son finally in the Chair of Classics. On 11 April 1948 Edward died from duodenal ulcers, at the age of seventy-seven.

In the department, new staff were being appointed. Bruce Harris, student at Auckland in the late 1930s, Senior Scholarship winner in Greek and Latin and Rhodes Scholar, was appointed lecturer in 1950 and remained with the department until appointed to Macquarie University, New South Wales, in 1970. With two full-time lecturers in the department, Blaiklock was now free to take his first sabbatical leave since joining the department in 1927.

In 1951 he visited England and the United States. Blaiklock and Kathleen planned to make it a family affair, taking both Peter and David with them. Peter was working with the YMCA and David was about to start in the fifth form at Mt Albert Grammar. Peter had become very friendly with a young lady (who later became his wife) and, deciding not to risk being out of the country for the best part of the year, remained at home. David went.

They spent six weeks in Sydney with Blaiklock fulfilling speaking engagements, and then went on to England. For the first time Blaiklock had been asked to speak at the famous Lake District Keswick Convention. World-famous preachers were speakers at Keswick and the invitation to Blaiklock signalled his becoming known and accepted internationally.

While in England, they stayed at the home of an elderly Irish couple in Essex. Dr and Mrs Beattie owned and managed a nursing home and were also pastors of an independent Baptist church that had been established largely through their own efforts. They lived in a centuries-old English manor first built in 1309 and reputed to be haunted by ghosts. On the darkest of nights, it was claimed, a chiming clock and other noises could be heard coming from the attic. David was still trying to work out his own faith and the time spent in the 'haunted' house produced more doubts and uncertainties in his fifteen-year-old mind than previously.

In the many weeks the Blaiklocks were there no chiming clock was heard, but a bandstand fell halfway down the stairs for no logical reason and on one occasion a round tray in the hall followed Blaiklock into a room when he opened a door.

There had been three murders and two suicides in the house and the rope used in the last suicide, in 1938, still hung in the cellar. 'It's always getting in the way and I will have to move it,' Mrs Beattie would say. But the rope remained, at least for the duration of the Blaiklocks' stay.

At Keswick, Blaiklock met two famous American preachers, Donald Grey Barnhouse and Harold Ockenga, who both invited him and the family to their country. They accepted and Blaiklock spoke in Ockenga's large independent church in Boston. Barnhouse had an annual thirty-week church circuit for Bible study seminars and Blaiklock took over this Barnhouse ministry for two weeks.

In Chicago, Blaiklock met and talked with Stacey Woods, International Secretary for the Inter-Varsity Fellowship.

The family returned home in November 1951. David went back to Mt Albert Grammar School in 1952, the only disadvantage from his year's leave was that he no longer qualified for having his matriculation examination accredited. However, he sat the examination that year and passed.

For the next year student numbers in Blaiklock's department were down on those of the previous year. This had come about through Latin 1 no longer being a required subject for law students. In one sense this removed a burden from the department as the majority of law students, with one or two exceptions, sought only a pass in Latin 1. Another contributory factor was the new education trend which modified the syllabus in secondary schools, encouraging social subjects at the expense of classics.

Blaiklock disapproved of the trend away from the traditional linguistic and literary approach to the classics. He saw the decision to abandon Latin 1 for law students as a factor in the long-term decline of Latin in academic schools. In his annual report to the University Council in 1952, he spoke of concern for the fact 'that the more poorly endowed have secured by continual agitation, a major modification in a course of university study. It is unlikely that example will pass unnoticed.'

Blaiklock had returned home considerably refreshed but with indications his duodenal ulcers would soon need being attended to. Shortly after his fiftieth birthday in 1954, Blaiklock underwent surgery for his recurring duodenal ulcers.

> It was a case for cool decision and I chose the drastic remedy which was the vogue in those days. I finished the second term, packing the year's work densely into the months before August and faced the unpleasant choice. I lost four days in pain and pethidine-haunted dreams for they almost killed me. But the reward which came with the ultimate healing was stable health for the rest of my life. The body amazingly adjusts to immense replumbing.
> (*Between the Foothills and the Ridge*, p. 72)

The operation was a complete success and at the start of the next university year, Blaiklock was glad to be back to full days in the department. Staff had been increased by the appointment of Dr H R Minn. An honours student in Latin and French from Otago University, he had secured a Teachers' diploma from the University of London, had lectured in classics at Otago and later, part-time at Sydney University while he had been tutor at Moore Theological College.

Blaiklock was glad he had taken his operation when he had, as in 1955, the whole university faced one of the periods of greatest change and upheaval in its history. It included the bitter site issue, which became a major public controversy, the Vietnam War protests and a spy scandal in which an SIS agent posed as a student to gather information on alleged communist students.

One particular form of student entertainment in the middle 1950s was the lunch-hour debates with students pitted against lecturers on such light-hearted topics as 'Achilles was a Heel,' and 'Plato Led a Dog's Life.' Originally put on by the Classics Department, these debates quickly attracted students and staff from other departments. The student newspaper *Cracuum* reports one such debate in which Blaiklock acted as chairman. The debate was entitled: 'No Place for an Academic in New Zealand Society.'

The *Cracuum* reporter quoted brief extracts from three speakers. The first one said in preparation for the debate 'I consulted the *Greater Oxford Dictionary* – this is known as research. I then came to a conclusion – that is called logic, after which I decided that "academic" meant a member of a university, regarded abstractly as the embodiment of mental states.

'The second speaker,' continued the *Cracuum* report, 'appealed to the sense of logic latent in the audience by producing two water-tight arguments, each one of which conclusively disproved the other. New Zealanders, she purred confidently, will soon reach such a state of cosy cushioned coma that all they will have to do is make plans and discuss them.

'The last speaker produced yet another slant on the subject – the fiendish. Walking feverishly round the lectern with a spine-chilling feline grace and the smile of the irrational fanatic, he brought home to the audience the truth of the phrase, "there's method in his madness". The New Zealander, he said, had the opportunity of creating absolutely tormenting questions that will never be solved. The purpose of the academic mind was to instill doubt and reveal not one or two but an infinity of sides to every question.'

Then the reporter waxed eloquent about the chairman:

> The result was exceptional because it was a draw with the aid of the chairman's casting vote . . . The chairman was exceptional firstly because he was Professor Blaiklock and secondly the most biased, prejudiced, amusing and thoroughly enjoyable

person ever to take the chair. It is hard to say whether he, or the three members of the staff team combined, were highest in the audience's favour.

Such participation shows Blaiklock's sense of humour and his ability to get alongside students in their fun times as well as in times of serious study. It also reveals something of a patronising attitude; how, from an implied position of intellectual superiority, the chairman, or the superior fatherly figure, quietly delights in having a laugh at the expense of his students.

Blaiklock's personal involvement with students went beyond the confines of the university. Kathleen was an excellent hostess and students were entertained regularly at the Titirangi home. Kathleen's upbringing on the Kent farm during the First World War when the Mitchell family had entertained New Zealand soldiers had been an excellent training ground.

All through their married lives the Blaiklocks welcomed students and friends to their home. During the Second World War, while they lived in Weston Avenue, this had included American soldiers. At Titirangi in the 1950s, two professors from Sydney University and the American evangelist Dr Billy Graham, when he visited New Zealand in 1959, were among the many visitors.

Three Auckland University professors, with whom Blaiklock had developed close, personal friendships, were also often entertained at Koromiko Road. They were Allwyn Keys, Professor of Modern Languages, Harold Rodwell, Associate Professor of Economics and Geoffrey Davis, Professor of Law.

At the university, the four often met over lunch in Professor Keys' study, usually at 'arpist', Geoffrey Davis' delightful expression for 12.30 p.m. Their topics of conversation were general chitchat about colleagues, criticising or commending institutions and individuals and generally putting the world to rights. Professor Keys used to remind Blaiklock good humouredly that he had won a scholarship in Greek which Blaiklock hadn't. Weather permitting, their discussions were frequently prolonged by leisurely strolls round the block, down the now vanished O'Rorke Street, Symonds Street, Waterloo Quadrant and back to Princes Street. On other occasions the lunch-time walk would begin and end at Grafton Road after a complete round of the Domain.

In mid-October, soon after lectures had ceased and before the onset of examinations, the professors would make excursions to Titirangi. Generally they travelled via Godley Road to the foreshore of the Manukau Harbour in the area of Green Bay where Blaiklock had roamed as a boy. Following the kindling of a fire on the beach and drinking their billy tea, Blaiklock would nostalgically recall incidents of his boyhood days.

Professor Keys remembers:

> The encroachment of modern buildings and speculators never failed to arouse a certain bitterness and resentment in him. I have often wondered whether this very sincere attachment to the whole area of Titirangi, the Waitakeres and the West Coast was the reason he became such an ardent New Zealander. I do not ever remember him speaking nostalgically of the place where he was born.
>
> Judging by what I have since learned and experienced of Birmingham, which in spite of its importance and amenities, is admittedly less attractive than many other cities I could name, I am still surprised that he passed it over so completely. Another curious omission was any reference to his mother, whereas references to his hard-working father were numerous and affectionate.

As often as possible, Blaiklock would take visitors on 'guided tours' through the Titirangi bush or along the Manukau Harbour foreshore, recounting stories of his boyhood days as they went. Meals would be served under the young kauri trees on their property and the sumptuous fare specially prepared by Kathleen would be appreciated.

Conversation at these times rarely revolved around the classics but it inevitably did include the environment. Few visitors left after a visit to Koromiko Road without being impressed afresh with the beauty of the Waitakere Range bush and landscape, more knowledgeable about native trees and plants and in greater sympathy with Blaiklock's desire to see the area preserved and protected from the ravages of an encroaching urbanisation.

It was a delightful environment for the boys to be brought up in, and when David went to Dunedin to qualify at the Medical School in 1956, home still remained the most exciting place in the world for him.

Blaiklock had always had an intense, compelling interest in medicine and lived out some of this in his son David and later in his granddaughter Alison, who also became a doctor.

It was Kathleen who corresponded regularly with David while he studied in Dunedin, but David has some letters from his father, written in his own handwriting and cryptic style in 1956:

Dear Davie,
Your letter arrived five minutes ago and I hasten to answer to relieve your doubts. I shall not for a moment doubt that you have done your best. I have a conviction that all will be well . . . You have six pounds eleven shillings and sixpence interest in your bank book.

Dear Davie,
First an educational section. Twice you have written 'through' for 'threw'. You must know that this is incorrect. Then you write 'traumour' for 'trauma'. This is Greek for a wound – a traumatic experience. I'm glad you are so happy; much of God's dealing with you is working out into the pattern of a plan. Perhaps you are not meant for academic medicine but have a very useful future in clinical medicine after all. But you'll cut your future short if you run on icy footpaths. You could get a nasty concussion or cracked bone. Be thankful for your good covering of flesh.

The 1950s was a very full decade for Blaiklock at university, at home as the boys grew into manhood, and in his growing non-university activities. His regular writing for magazines and newspapers continued and, following the link he had established with the Barnhouse organisation in Philadelphia, he began writing regularly for *Eternity*

*Magazine*. Later in the decade when the magazine *Christianity Today* was established in the United States, independent of the Billy Graham Organisation but theologically one with it, he began writing for that too.

But it was his writing commission in 1959 for the Scripture Union which laid the foundation for him in religious books which he authored particularly throughout the 1960s. For five years, from 1959 to 1963 inclusive, Blaiklock wrote the *Daily Notes* for the Scripture Union.

> The Daily Notes in most cases are the material of morning devotion among thousands of busy people caught in the rush of a great city's life, strap-hanging on the Tube, packed in commuter trains to Cannon Street or Charing Cross, shepherding in the Highlands, weaving the traffic on Sydney Harbour Bridge – a thousand situations before and during busy days. They even penetrate the mission fields.

His comments covered the whole Bible, averaging 225 words daily. His brief was to write instructively and challengingly and with an expository and devotional slant.

His first contribution for Thursday 1 January 1959 set the standard. His commentary for this day was on Psalm 103:

> This famous and moving Psalm begins the year on the note of joyous praise. Three times at the beginning, four times at the end, David calls for praise. The body of the Psalm reveals the old spiritual maturity of the Old Testament revelation. Here, indeed, is the God and Father of our Lord Jesus Christ – forgiving, redeeming, loving, tender, mightily just, merciful, gracious, paternal, pitying, true. The singer exhausts the vocabulary of his language in his endeavour to set forth a God more gentle, understanding and compassionate than any earthly father and able utterly and absolutely to forgive. David had known in bitter experience the need for that mercy and had grasped it with both hands. The Christian and biblical view of God has won acceptance. Wherever the Gospel has been preached, even those who do not accept it, think of God, if they think at all, as good, merciful, a Father to men. Not so in the pagan world, past and present, where evil powers have masqueraded as divine. The Bible and the Christ of the Bible,

tore the mask from such devilish deceit and in so doing, left rebellious man without excuse.

Blaiklock's final contribution, written for Tuesday 31 December 1963, was again back in the Psalms. In the five years he had been writing the *Daily Notes*, he received correspondence from readers in many countries. When this writing period ended, the letters came in their hundreds. Commenting later on the type of letters he received, relating to other writings as well as the *Daily Notes*, Blaiklock says:

> My correspondents have been many . . . most of them have had pleasant words to say, a few have been hostile, others have caught me in error, always a delight to some . . . One should be grateful for such critics. They make for care and alertness . . . but one does wish the corrector would suppress the note of jubilation.
> 
> (*Between the Foothills and the Ridge*, p. 70)

Some years later he again traversed the whole Bible for the Scripture Union, writing studies this time on the characters of the Bible.

> Such a task involved me with great men, Abraham, Moses, David, Paul, Peter – Abraham daunting in his vision of the task which obsessed him, the gift, not less of a true God, a holy God to the world of man; Moses, heir of two cultures, nobly surrendering all to free a nation and to give them, along with liberty, justice, a destiny and a vision; David, peptic, passionate rising to sublime heights of insight and fumbling, tumbling to nether hells; Paul, one of all history's massive intellects who knew how to weave the legacy of three dynamic peoples into a single culture and a unique cementing faith; Peter, a fisherman, faulty, human, who led a band of simple men towards the conquest of the world . . . I observed the ruthless truth with which the Bible, from the patriarchs to the apostles, recorded them, making one and all recognisable in their flawed, as well as in the noble shapes and colours of their humanity. It became as I read and wrote my 425 words on each, or on one fact of each man and woman, another demonstration of the Book's true humanity.
> 
> (*The Bible and I*, p. 95–96)

These writings on the Bible and its characters, increased Blaiklock's knowledge and love for the scriptures as a whole and convinced him of the Bible's revelation for mankind and its relevance to the evolving history of the world. He saw the Old Testament as the story of a nation with a unique destiny in that history. Of Israel, he wrote

> Here was a nation born to destiny, bound together and to history by a task, born in liberty, falling, rising, failing, triumphing, shaped by suffering as well as by success, beating out a view of life, divided yet one, scattered yet united, the mother of great men living in the native land of Christ, the producer of the interwoven Testaments. True, one can follow the Greeks from Homer to Hellenism, from Athens to Alexandria; Rome can be viewed from the claustrophobic drive from a Tiber enclave to an empire stretching from Hadrian's wall to the Persian Gulf . . . but nothing parallels Abraham to Christ and their binding story.
> 
> (*The Bible and I*, p. 97)

Blaiklock was also continuing with writing editorials, book reviews and Grammaticus articles for *New Zealand Herald* publications.

In 1960 David More arrived from England to take a position on the *Herald*'s literary staff. Later in the year he became literary editor. An Englishman with a classical background and a love for Latin literature in particular, More had much in common with Blaiklock. They became firm friends for life. More was impressed with Blaiklock's literary style:

> His Grammaticus essays showed his personal gift for combining great scholarship with popular appeal, a rare achievement. There can be hardly any subject on which he did not touch. He wrote on trees, especially his beloved kauris, on insects, birds, social manners, history, the literature of many nations, the seasons, the New Zealand and English countrysides, flying, countries he had visited and on innumerable other subjects. Like Shakespeare, there was no respect of human life which to him remained without investigation and comment.

Through his long association with Blaiklock and Kathleen, More saw characteristics of Blaiklock other than those seen by friends and acquaintances. Although he had a capacious memory, Blaiklock often failed to verify his quotations. In one of his autobiographies he headed a chapter: 'And when they take to feeling old,' a line altered from Rupert Brooke's poem about Granchester. When More pointed this out, Blaiklock replied:

> You ought to know by now that I refuse to check quotations. In a lifetime with lower criticism, I have always given the writer the benefit of the better word. That is why I sometimes unconsciously make an amendation. Brooke should have been ashamed to use 'get'. Like 'thing', it is one of those vulgar little words I never use, save in the rarest literary contexts . . . Kipling can often be improved upon. His education was not remarkable.

More found Blaiklock's beliefs on women, more in keeping with ancient times than the twentieth century. Blaiklock believed the prime function of a woman was to minister to the well-being of her husband. And Kathleen, for whom all Blaiklock's associates had a warm regard and affection, undoubtedly lived up to his ideal. But with Blaiklock's predominantly liberal outlook, More found it strange that he tended to judge women rather by their sexual morality than by other qualities, especially their artistic or intellectual achievements.

In one of his articles, Blaiklock wrote of Clodia, usually identified as the Lesbia of Catullus' verse, as 'worthless'. (Clodia was a courtesan who tormented Catullus but she did inspire some of his most memorable poetry.) More queried Blaiklock's description of her as 'useless'. To him it seemed uncharacteristic of a committed Christian writer who believed that no human spirit was worthless. Blaiklock agreed he might have been too hard but emphasised that Clodia was a thoroughly bad woman.

More found Blaiklock ready with excuses for his heroes who had gone astray through the wiles of women and not, he suggested, through their own stupidity or wickedness.

He classed 'the scheming little solo Nell Gwyn, with the cunning Bathsheba,' and added: 'Poor old David, he was a great soldier and poet.'

Another battle of words and ideas took place between them when More contended that King Charles II was the best monarch England had ever had. The king had many mistresses, he was witty, intelligent, interested in science and the arts and, in an intolerant age, relatively tolerant, More claimed. In reply, Blaiklock wrote: 'I can never understand your admiration for that slimy tomcat Charles Stuart. Like his smelly pal over the Channel, Louis XIV, he was a peril to his country. France did not survive him; it lurched on to the Revolution. England did – thanks to the Authorised Version.'

More considered this clearly showed Blaiklock's opinion of Charles was coloured more by the king's sexual life than by his other qualities. Such an attitude to sex was the hallmark of the Puritan – and Blaiklock admired the Puritan ethic. When challenged with being intolerant, Blaiklock denied strenuously that he was. His father, he said, had drummed into him: 'We owe the world a debt of tolerance.'

But there was no doubt, More feels, that occasionally a slight undertone of bitterness crept into Blaiklock's writing and conversation. His beliefs gave him a lack of sympathy – and that is a euphemism – for some pleasures of hundreds of thousands of New Zealanders.

On one occasion he expressed annoyance at being impeded on the footpath by a crowd waiting to buy lottery tickets. On another, he called jockeys at a race meeting, 'crouching gnomes'. More asked if he would have been equally annoyed when hindered by a crowd waiting to enter a prayer meeting? Would he have applied the same contemptuous epithet to the prayer-meeting participants who adopted the same posture as the jockeys? Was it coincidence that Anglicans and Roman Catholics referred to the Free Church attitude of prayer as 'the Presbyterian crouch'? Blaiklock never answered the first two questions but referring to the 'crouch', and though a Baptist, replied: 'Yes, horrible. I fit the Anglican role very well.'

Kindly and in no sense judgementally, More noticed

other anomalies in Blaiklock. For example, in his Grammaticus column, Blaiklock denounced atmospheric pollution and the pall of smoke hanging over Auckland. Yet he wrote charmingly (and More considered rightly so) about the pleasures of his own open fire and was pleased when a friend sent him a present of coal. He pleaded in compensation the fact that he had planted more trees.

Or again, in academic circles the cult and mystique of wine seems inseparable from a classicist, observed More. The popular sentiment is of dons talking long and learnedly over their port and of Hilare Belloc, that scholar and author who ascribed to wine everything of value in European civilisation and who viewed vineyards with lyric joy: yet Blaiklock was a teetotaller.

Editor of the *New Zealand Herald*, 'Budge' Hintz said Blaiklock always kept a number of timeless and undatable articles for his Grammaticus column in reserve. This was in case he was ill, on holiday or overseas.

It was unusual, he said, for a classical scholar to contribute regularly for so long to newspaper publications and especially to win so many enthusiastic readers. The reasons why Blaiklock achieved this, Hintz believed, was because

> Blaiklock never wrote down to the lowest common denominator of human intelligence. He believed that anyone intelligent enough to read and comprehend clean print, carefully and sympathetically constructed would respond with widened mental horizons. This is precisely what happened. Letters from readers came in their thousands.
>
> He was one of the few who learned much from history and who applied that learning to the affairs of our own day. His essays, with their background of inspiration from the ancient classics, disclosed an abiding love for his adopted land. He was 'Brummagem born' but from early childhood became a devoted New Zealander ever conscious of the beauty of the land and the essential friendliness of the majority of its people.
>
> He did not write for the activist, the self-righteous, the rebels or other misfits in our society. He wrote for those with a yearning, conscious or sub-conscious, for the melody of words and the rhythm of reasons. He strove constantly for what Ivor

Brown had described as 'the apt, the brief, the memorable phrase'. Those of my calling who knew him (they usually referred to him affectionately as 'Dr Ted' or 'the Prof') will always remember with gratitude, his gifts to a profession he graced with his abundant talents.

Hintz also acknowledged that it was Blaiklock who 'inspired some of us to do something for the preservation and protection of our heritage in a lovely land. With all his erudite reflections on classical literature, Blaiklock was a modern conservationist in the best sense of the word.

Blaiklock had now moved well on from his solitary days managing the Greek section only, when new staff for the department had all been attached to Latin. Now they were appointed where needed most and staff numbers under his regime eventually grew to eight.

In 1963 two new appointments were made possible by a more generous staffing policy the university was able to adopt. W F Richardson was a former student and winner of Senior Scholarships in Greek and Latin in 1960. After a Cambridge degree he returned immediately to Auckland and to a position with the department (In 1977 he won a Ph.D. from the University of Otago.)

In 1963 also, two stages of Biblical History and Literature were introduced by the Classics Department. The call for biblical study to be included as part of the university curriculum was first raised in an article in the student newspaper *Cracuum* of 8 July 1957. It was taken up by the SCM and theological students. The new subject, introduced in two stages, was a partial adjunct of Ancient History and Biblical History and Literature. Two of the department's staff were best qualified to prepare the course: with Blaiklock, Harris and Minn carried it through. Its introduction led weight to the efforts of the department to improve staff-student ratios with the appointment of two additional staff in 1963.

Blaiklock played his full part in the general life of the university. In the days of the University of New Zealand (Auckland University gained its autonomy in 1962), he was a member of the Academic Board, the Entrance Board and the Senate. While still a lecturer, he was president of the Lecturers' Association and lecturers' representative on the Professorial Board. He became Dean of the Faculty of Arts in 1949 and also served as a University Council member, a University representative, sat on the Grammar School Board and was a member of the State Literary Fund Advisory Committee. In 1964 Blaiklock took his last sabbatical leave, spending it with Kathleen in the Middle East, Greece, Italy, Britain and the United States. In 1965, in recognition of his literary and oratorical skills, Blaiklock was appointed the University of Auckland's first public orator.

Also in 1965, Blaiklock's thirty-eight year association with the Bible College of New Zealand was honoured by his being appointed president and chairman of the College Board in succession to Robert Laidlaw.

The association had begun in 1927 when Blaiklock had been lecturing in Latin and Greek at the Auckland University. The College, then called the Bible Training Institute (BTI), had been founded by Rev Joseph Kemp, minister at the Auckland Baptist Tabernacle.

In the jubilee issue of the *Reaper* (1922–72), the official organ of the college, Blaiklock wrote of the early days of the Institute when it was in the city:

> It was in 1927 that I first tried to persuade the students that Greek was an easier language than most others they might be called on to learn. That was the year I first began teaching Classics in the University. I looked forward to Friday mornings. I commonly finished a University lecture at 10 o'clock and walked through the park and up Queen Street to spend the rest of the morning at the Institute. There was J O Sanders, my own contemporary (later to become Institute Principal) to talk to and Kemp, a breezy presence at morning tea, his conversation full of a hundred anecdotes, and above all, the students . . .

Blaiklock was always proud of his close association with the Bible College which he regarded as 'impeccably conservative, second to none in the standards of its scholarship and . . . a dominant influence in the Church in New Zealand' (*The Bible and I*, p. 83).

In the jubilee issue of the *Reaper* he also wrote of the college as follows:

> If one group in this distracted world can claim that it is not to be blamed for the ills which afflict mankind, it is those Christians who have stood firm by Biblical Christianity. In the work and teaching of the College we have held fast to . . . 'an informed conservatism'. We have seen no need to diminish the authority of the Scripture or to demote its Christ. We have always sought to show where those unnecessary intrusions of rationalism would lead and that there was no clear sticking point on the path which led from liberalism to atheism.

Rev David Stewart was appointed principal of the College in 1965. He had an M.Sc., B.A. and B.D. from Sydney University where he was also a Gold Medallist. His appointment followed his eleven years in India where he had been headmaster of the Mt Hermon School in Darjeeling.

He had been approached about submitting an application for the vacant position at the college and recalls visiting Auckland for an interview. On arrival he was met first by a triumverate from the college – the then chairman, Robert Laidlaw; Alec Bain and Ted Blaiklock. They considered it appropriate they should talk with him before he met the full board.

Soon after David Stewart's appointment, Blaiklock became president, succeeding Robert Laidlaw. 'Blaiklock was always a very strong principal's man and closely associated with me from that time,' David Stewart says. 'It was a principle for him that he should do everything possible to build up the position of the principal and this he certainly did for me. I was aware other people had their differences with him but I never did. He was a warm friend and always encouraging to me.'

Blaiklock could not have become president at a more appropriate time for the college. The move from the top of Queen Street to new property and buildings in Lincoln Road, Henderson, had been completed and the name changed. He followed one of New Zealand's leading businessmen and when appointed, remarked: 'I don't understand business, it's not my interest. I can't contribute anything in that area.'

Business expertise, however, was not now as pressing a need as it had been during the planning, financing and building of the new Bible College premises. On the academic side, Blaiklock felt he had a distinctive contribution to make.

David Stewart observes: 'In the earlier years of the Institute, the policy had been almost deliberately non-academic.' It was over-cautious, an attempt not to do anything that a theological college did.

But something had to be done for students who weren't seeking a training for Church ministry but were wanting one equally as good, academically. 'It was only after we moved to Henderson that we began doing external diplomas and degrees,' continues David Stewart. 'So it was exactly the right time for Blaiklock – much more appropriate than ten years earlier in the middle of a new building programme and major move of premises.'

Blaiklock suggested having a president's hour once a week. For this he had the whole college and periodically introduced a session in which students could submit written questions. Stewart remembers that, 'In his own inimitable way, Blaiklock worked right through the Psalms. He didn't take them as strictly academic subjects but applied them to the lives of the individuals. Some of his periods were deeply meaningful. Through these periods in particular, he became very well known to the students.'

The president's faith, according to David Stewart, was a very intellectual one. Though it did not lack emotion – Blaiklock was a very emotional person – his emotion was always related to understanding and thought. For example, he found it very difficult to accept that dancing could have anything to do with worship. Although Blaiklock later mellowed in this respect when the trend became universal, he was never in favour of any form of drama being used in a church service.

Blaiklock also found it hard to accept women in church leadership roles. Until his retirement, the College Board was comprised exclusively of men. Blaiklock was not the instigator of this unwritten policy but there was no thought of it being changed during his chairmanship. When the question did occasionally arise, it was gently and conveniently 'pushed under the carpet'. Blaiklock took his basis for the role of women in the church from Romans 16:1–2, 'I commend to you our sister Phoebe, a deaconess of the church at Cenchreae . . . for she has been a helper of many and of myself as well.' Blaiklock saw Kathleen in the biblical picture of Phoebe and 'into it she fitted so perfectly', says David Stewart. But he was always hesitant about women who sought a leadership role in the church.

Blaiklock's closest friend at the university, Professor Geoffrey Davis, died in England in May 1966. He had been appointed Professor of Law in 1942 and had retired in 1964. With Mrs Davis he had visited relatives in England and died while there. Professor and Mrs Keys also visited England later in the year. During a conversation with Blaiklock on their return, they showed him a photo of them both outside the lovely old parish church of St Andrew at Clyton, Devon, where Professor Davis' funeral service had been held. Professor Keys says he was surprised at the time to 'almost feel the resentment of loyalty in Ted's mind, that we, not he, had been able to pay homage to the memory of a very dear friend'.

## 8   CONTENDING FOR THE FAITH

Blaiklock was never one to seek controversy but in 1965 he was pressed by students to take part in a debate, at Auckland Training College, on Christianity versus atheism.

Head of the University of Auckland's Philosophy Department, Professor R D Bradley was the speaker on atheism. He had earlier attended the Mt Albert Baptist Church but had become a militant atheist, holding anti-Christian views with a fervour to match Blaiklock's evangelical zeal. Students welcomed the debate by two of their professors with diametrically opposed views on life and death.

Professor Bradley was the first to speak. He began by retelling the story originally told by the English philosopher, Antony Flew, when the latter sought to make a point for atheism. This was playing right into Blaiklock's hands; he was familiar with the story, the weakness of it being that it could easily be extended and answered.

The illustration was of two men lost in a forest. In the midst of their predicament, they came across what appeared to be a garden. They stumbled across paths, garden beds, patches of flowers and vegetables. It was obvious somebody had been at work.

One of them said to his companion: 'There must be a gardener here. There must be somebody about.' The other replied: 'Can you see the gardener, can you hear him?' They made every effort to find the gardener, devising tests to catch him out, but all to no avail. The first man, still convinced there was a gardener somewhere, decided he must be invisible, intangible, elusive but existing. He continued tending the garden. He took little notice of his companion's sceptical remarks: 'In what way does your, invisible, inaudible, absent gardener differ from no gardener at all?' Professor Bradley produced this question with a decisive flourish. It was the high point of his case.

In his turn, Blaiklock carried on with the Antony Flew story: 'One day when the first man was working alone in the garden, down the path came a sturdy, handsome man,' Blaiklock said. As the working man looked up, the unexpected visitor said to him: 'I hear you are puzzled about the gardener and are looking for him. Take a good look at me. I am the gardener's son, and they say, I am in all respects like my father.'

In a sense, this is what happens with the Christian, Blaiklock continued, pointing out the absurdity of Antony Flew's argument. Just because something can't be seen, felt, heard or smelt does not mean it does not exist. Blaiklock pointed to the bush, the trees, all creation and every fragment of everything living as evidence that 'a mind has been at work'. It must be a daunting mind, he continued, a mind beyond comprehension, so marvellous, so superior to our own we are naturally puzzled and frightened by it. But when God put himself into human form in his Son Jesus Christ and when he comes 'walking up the garden path' to meet us and says: 'Look at me, I am exactly like my Father,' we have some means of grasping the whole concept. Accepting that God was in Christ, it is possible to understand the love of God by the love of Christ.

The addresses of the debate were recorded on tape and there was considerable demand for them. As a sequel, Blaiklock edited a book, published by Zondervans, *Why I am Still a Christian*, in which eleven academics from several countries contributed. They included a philosopher, a medical doctor, two physicists, a biochemist, a geographer, a scientist, an anatomist and a musician.

One of the contributors was John A McIntyre, Professor of Physics at The Texas A&M University, USA. In a letter to Blaiklock, dated 23 June 1971, he wrote:

> This is just a note to say how much I have enjoyed reading your book *Why I am Still a Christian*. Ignoring the fact that I am a contributor, I consider this book in a class by itself for its charm and persuasiveness. One cannot but be impressed by the range

of appeal that Jesus Christ has to all men. While your Christians are all scholars, they nevertheless represent a wide spectrum of humanity in their apprehension of Christ. Their scholarly bond serves in this book primarily to insure that each essay will appeal to the young student for whom this collection is so clearly appropriate. My own personal comment is to say how honoured I am to be included in such distinguished company. I know the Lord will use this book and I want to thank you for making it available to the thinking person.

Blaiklock's own contribution to the book included a delightful paragraph on how it is possible to know a person of another age:

I became a Christian as a student through an encounter with Christ. Let no one tell me with the slick logic in fashion today that the phrase is meaningless. It is possible in real experience to meet and know a person of another age. Lucretius met Epicurus, who died two centuries before Lucretius was born and the encounter changed his life. I think I know Euripides and Vergil, the two poets over whom I have pondered for years as a teacher of Greek and Latin, well enough to be at ease with both upon a dozen themes, if some time-machine could take me back to their age. And tens of millions have met Christ and known transformation.

In the early 1960s, a 'new theology' purporting to be a giant step forward for men in his religious questings, had hit the headlines in the United States, Great Britain and became a public issue in New Zealand in 1966. At the heart of debate raised by the 'new theology' were the basic doctrines of Christianity, the divinity of Christ – particularly his resurrection.

According to Professor Lloyd Geering, principal of the Presbyterian Church of New Zealand's Knox Theological College, Dunedin, faith was independent of doctrine. The early disciples who believed in the resurrection of Christ had had a subjective or 'discernment' experience, not one based on what history could affirm as fact.

For the conservative Christian, a faith not based on the essential doctrines such as the resurrection, was not a 'faith unto salvation', whatever else it might be.

In an article in the Easter 1966 issue of *Outlook*, the official publication of the Presbyterian Church, Professor Geering sought to sketch the difficulty of relating the resurrection narratives of the New Testament to the kind of world in which we live and to show that in spite of these the resurrection faith of the church can still have meaning for the men who have left behind the world view of the first century . . . we may freely say that the bones of Jesus lie somewhere in Palestine . . . Christian faith is not destroyed by the admission. On the contrary, only now, when this has been said, are we in a position to ask about the meaning of the resurrection as an integral part of the message concerning Jesus.

In November 1967, a group within the Presbyterian Church pressed heresy charges against Professor Geering, which were dismissed. Professor Geering later resigned and was appointed Professor of Religious Studies at the Victoria University, Wellington.

Blaiklock was not personally involved in these events but when Geering published his views in a book *God in the New World*, Blaiklock was urged, as a classical scholar, to write a rebuttal. A publisher agreed to Blaiklock writing *Layman's Answer* and he was given six weeks to complete the manuscript.

In his book, a philosophical treatise, Geering described faith as being independent of both knowledge and doctrine. His emphasis was on the 'Christ of Faith', not the 'Jesus of History'. Quotations from his *God in the New World* are as follows:

> All human knowledge is subject to further correction and change and must be adhered to with some degree of tentativeness, however small. It may be likened to the frozen surface of a pond. Just because it will support a skater one day, there is no guarantee that it will do the next (p. 27).
> Doctrines or formulated beliefs are neither to be identified with faith nor regarded as the origin of faith. Doctrines result from faith and constitute the expression of faith for a limited historical period. These doctrines can come and go. Sometimes what

has been an orthodox doctrine for some long time has to be discarded (p. 139).

Many people in the new world have abandoned active commitment to the Christian heritage not because they wanted to but because the church led them to believe that the Christian faith was to be identified with certain dogmatic statements which for them no longer had the ring of truth. We must go behind doctrines and beliefs if we are to understand the origin and meaning of faith (p. 140).

. . . Indeed, if the life of Jesus is to be related to God in any way at all, then we are forced to move out of the language of history and enter the medium of myth. For the historian per se can say nothing about God. The historian may elaborate the evidence relating to the empty tomb but Peter's statement of faith, 'This Jesus God raised up', is outside the scope of historical enquiry (p. 145).

Blaiklock said he had six reasons for writing *Layman's Answer*. They were:

1: Principal Geering's (to me) uninformed assumption that all New Testament scholars share his views and agnosticism.
2: The damage done to language and communication by his popularization of the 'double talk' of the New Theology – a misuse of speech traceable back to Renan, a century ago, but made common, and the cause of wide confusion by a minority of modern theologians.
3: In protest against the arrogance by which agnosticism, which once honestly withdrew from the church, remains within the church to sabotage and mislead.
4: To offer a reasonable presentation of the historic faith in terms acceptable to modern man but without debilitating loss of content.
5: In the belief that a classical scholar, familiar with the period, the background and the language of the New Testament, is uniquely qualified to say something authoritative about its documents.
6: In the hope that fallacious views of history, evident throughout Principal Geering's book, will be adequately refuted. The book *God in the New World* contains no new idea. Every alleged innovation can be traced back a century and in some cases (e.g. the distinction of 'the Jesus of history' and the Christ of faith) for nineteen centuries. Nor is the world, save in the products of invention, 'new'.

Blaiklock wrote his book under the following chapter headings: 'No New World', 'The Heart of Christianity', 'The Documents in the Case', 'Myth or History' (two chapters), 'The Resurrection in History', 'Faith in God', 'Faith in Christ', 'the Practice of Prayer', 'Man and his Destiny', 'The Question of Death', 'What of the Future?'

As a result of the controversy, the question of the resurrection of Christ, in particular, became strongly debated in the popular press, over the radio and on television. The *New Zealand Herald*, published a review of *Layman's Answer*, contributed by John Morton, Professor of Zoology at the University, Auckland.

> ... Given my broad accord with Professor Blaiklock's position, I have to ask whether he has given an answer that churchmen will find widely acceptable. Do I – as a Catholic and a scientist, find the shallowness of Professor Geering countered by the rigidity, however eloquent, of an evangelical Baptist? This is a query with which many will open the book and it is one, I believe, Professor Blaiklock survives with credit.
>
> There is no fundamentalism here, only concern with fundamentals. The author's style is as distinguished as old friends of Grammaticus would expect and he has a copious command of documents and contemporary illustration. Anglicans will find this more a preaching book than they may be accustomed to. There is little of the detachment of academic theologians and the author himself realises that reticence has been difficult. 'There are times of brash challenge when a Christian must speak.'
>
> But Professor Blaiklock is never careless of scholarship and his fluency in the New Testament is widely acknowledged. Often with biblical authorship and criticism he will choose a conservative statement where an alternative view might validly be open.
>
> In the chapter 'No New World', he discounts the contemporary assumption that we are in a new era with cavemen and Plato and Michelangelo on one side of the divide and ourselves, come of age, on the other. Professor Geering's 'New World' is indeed a dangerous generalisation on which to demolish the theology of a transcendant God. There is at least nothing said by biology or physics to cause a panic abandonment of traditional beliefs. And nothing to loosen the belief

that man is a creature in revolt against his Creator and in desperate need of a redeemer.

Professor Blaiklock affirms that God has revealed himself in Christ in a way that gives men sufficient knowledge of him and has confirmed the fact by raising the Crucified from the dead. To Geering, the Resurrection ('Christ is risen indeed') is a subjective state of exaltation and new-found strength. The first Christians had 'experienced a discernment situation'.

Blaiklock is entitled to ask if the new theologians are being honest with the documents. He leans strongly on W M Ramsay's powerful exposition of Luke as a most accurate and meticulous ancient historian. Geering and others, he holds to have been as sweeping about New Testament criticism as they have with statements about science and philosophy. 'No student of ancient literature other than in New Testament studies would feel free to meet the difficulty of our Lord's prophecy with the simple and effective procedure of excising the awkward words from the records. "I do not believe Jesus said those words" is a statement of personal unbelief, not necessarily a piece of scholarly criticism.'

The New Testament writers were clearly not trying to express a saving truth symbolically but describing a Resurrection they believed had happened in history. Geering claims these events are outside the field of reference of history. To Blaiklock and to many, this supposition would cast away the verity of a real Incarnation.

Whether or not historical methods are likely to throw new light on them, these truths are not invulnerable to history. We hold them at perilous risk of history and our faith is that they will stand this test. 'It is possible to gain an impression of the historical Jesus so tremendous that it daunts and overwhelms.' Blaiklock refers with effect to the wealth of evidence found in the lives and response of the apostles and the early Church. The real credibility gap would seem to be in squaring this with the antisupernatural view.

To be fair, there could be a wide alternative territory between Geering and the answer. What do we, or can we really mean by the 'objectivity' of a resurrected presence that appeared selectively to many but not all, that on several occasions clearly showed trans-natural properties and that – as Blaiklock would concede – must have been encountered under different modes by Paul on the Damascus road and Thomas in the upper room.

There is a vast area here in which the Church has wisely not sought to dogmatise about mechanics and metaphysics . . .

Blaiklock could firmly answer that the disappearance of a fleshy body from the tomb is an inseparable part of the whole transaction.

What effect will *Layman's Answer* have? It says more eloquently and comprehensively much that has been recently stressed. Yet the secularist current is strong today and *God in the New World* is as much a product as a cause of it. With a tribunal of contemporary New Zealanders, setting light to theology and history, Geering, appearing to defend his personal beliefs, would have a good jury. The Christianity of the Creeds is being called 'conservative' today but perhaps Blaiklock would regret this less than I.

But if our standpoint is a minority one, it has never in our own day been more bravely expressed: 'Unless Christ be risen, there is no Christianity, all hope is cut at the root, the foundation of all goodness sapped. "My Lord", said Thomas, "and my God". It echoes down the years and with passion in the affirmation, let us join with him in the making of it at the other end of history.'

Not everyone approved *Layman's Answer*. In a review in *The Christchurch Press*, Rev John Rymer, then Lecturer in the Philosophy of Religion at the University of Canterbury (now Dean of St Mary's Cathedral, Auckland), expressed his dissatisfaction with Blaiklock's effort. As an answer from the Bible, Rymer was impressed. He was concerned, however, that *Layman's Answer* did not deal with the philosophical questions Geering raised.

Others considered the book failed, from the strictly theological viewpoint, to answer Geering's theological questions. One of these was Dr Bob Thompson, former student of Blaiklock at the University, then lecturer at the Baptist Theological College and later to become its principal. (Dr Thompson later became Lecturer in Biblical and Historical Literature at Spurgeon's College, London.) At the time *Layman's Answer* appeared, Dr Thompson had just returned from a six-month visit to Israel. He wrote to Blaiklock pointing out 'a number of infelicities, especially in geographical errors with regard to the Holy Land', and then phoned him. According to Thompson, 'the telephone line was red-hot for a few minutes'.

Rev David Stewart, principal of the Bible College of New

Zealand, said *Layman's Answer* gave answers for the layman that were necessary but the book did not really grapple with the theological and philosophical questions Geering raised. Blaiklock wrote it under great pressure of time, David Stewart continued. Within himself Blaiklock had a certain feeling of anger about Geering: 'This man is destroying the hope of people who lose their loved ones and giving them nothing to replace it,' Blaiklock had remarked.

Ivan Moses, principal of the Auckland Technical Institute, a member of the Bible College of New Zealand's Board of Directors and later president of the college following Blaiklock's retirement, commented on Geering and Blaiklock's books as follows: 'They were like ships passing one another in the night. But *Layman's Answer* contributed immeasurably to stemming the flood of those leaving Christian churches as a result of the Geering controversy.'

A Rhodes Scholar with an MSc and a major in Greek from Auckland University, Rev Francis Foulkes was not in New Zealand at the time of the Geering controversy. (He later became lecturer at St John's Theological College, Auckland, and part-time Lecturer in Biblical History and Literature at the University of Auckland.) While overseas from 1949 to 1973, Foulkes kept closely in touch with Blaiklock. He admired his great love for the scriptures and his ability in both speaking and writing to make them live to the ordinary person,

> But in the more scholarly, academic circles, in biblical history and theology, it would be fair to say Blaiklock didn't grapple with the issues being debated in these areas . . .
> I think this is what prejudiced (if this is the right word), many of those who were not of the evangelical faith, against Blaiklock. I regretted some of the negative things he said, but basically, in my own understanding of biblical authority, I stand very close to him.

Blaiklock's great strength, according to Foulkes, was to help people understand the setting of the biblical world – the classical side of which many biblical scholars neglect.

By emphasizing this he helped make the Bible live; but he didn't grapple with the more theological aspects, or didn't feel it was his part to do so. Thus he did not dialogue or debate with those who held these views.

There was a sense in which it could be said he did enter into debate with Geering but it was almost like two lines that didn't meet. He answered the latter from the point of view of his own faith and his own area of scholarship but not in the area of the scholarship of Geering.

A review of Professor Geering's book in the weekly Catholic newspaper, *The Tablet*, of 1 May 1968, by an Old Testament scholar, strongly criticised Geering's scholarship. The reviewer was Rev Ian Sanders, Rector of the Catholic Holy Cross College, Mosgiel. Taking Geering's remark: 'It is sometimes argued . . .' Sanders quoted from nine other Old Testament scholars, each of whom disagreed with different points raised by Geering.

Sanders wrote:

> Considering the authors quoted above (and I could have quoted more), the alleged position of biblical scholarship expressed in the statement "It is sometimes argued," is a travesty on the part of a Professor of Old Testament studies.
>
> In criticising the book (*God in the New World*) so trenchantly, I have no wish in any way to question Professor Geering's sincerity. Nor do I doubt his desire to help others. Nevertheless I must repeat that in so far as he attempts to substantiate his case, he displays a singular lack of scholarship for a man of his position.

The Geering and Blaiklock books highlighted one of the greatest – if not the greatest – religious controversies in the short history of New Zealand. It was a major topic of debate throughout the latter years of the 1960s and was recalled briefly in an article in the *Listener* (the official publication of the New Zealand Broadcasting Corporation) of 18 August 1984. In an article introducing a television series produced on Blaiklock shortly before his death, journalist Vernon Wright quotes Dr Jim Veitch, of the Religious Studies Department at Victoria University, saying he believes Professor Blaiklock has probably had more impact on New Zealand's religious population than has Professor Geering. For instance, he thinks most Christians in New Zealand are probably what would be called conservative and that their majority in the churches is probably growing. Why? 'Because people are wanting to stand on as firm a ground as possible in a time when the ground is not very firm.'

# 9 STUDENTS SHOW THEIR APPRECIATION

Time at the university was beginning to run out for Blaiklock and it was his last Latin honours students of 1968 who endeared themselves to him in a unique way. The group consisted of four men and four women who relished turning every session into an opportunity for vigorous discussion. They carried on their association with Blaiklock until shortly before his death. This they did through a closed society called the Augustani, which met once a year for a meal with the Professor on the birthday of the first Roman emperor, Augustus (63 BC to AD 14) on (or as near as possible to) 21 September each year.

One of this group was Dr Vivienne Gray (nee Forbes and to become Senior Lecturer in Classics at the University of Auckland). She gives her impressions of Blaiklock as a lecturer, beginning from her first year in 1965, and recalls how the Augustani relationship began:

> For the Professor's lectures, we gathered early. He made his entrance at five past the hour, proceeding from his office, which adjoined the lecture room, down the slightly sloping aisle between the rows of desks and up to the rostrum and high stool on which he sat in front of the lectern.
> 
> He had the psychological advantage of entering behind our backs and having an eye-to-eye contact until he settled himself at the front. He could also that way, display to best advantage, the academic gown he usually wore for the first-year classes, since the slight slope allowed it an impressive billow or two on its journey to the rostrum.
> 
> I do not remember that he ever smiled at us; he merely looked up, from side to side, and began. It seemed that his entrance was stage managed: enter back right, proceed to

centre stage . . . I am sure he enjoyed it immensely. In later years, listening to our recollection of it, he did smile, in an embarrassed way.

He lectured most memorably on Catullus (?84–?54 BC, said to be the greatest lyric poet of Rome), Horace (65–8 BC, Roman poet) and Vergil (70–19 BC, the greatest Roman poet) with Tennyson wherever not absolutely inappropriate. His style of delivery was magnificent and made him one of the most attractive of lecturers. By the time I reached the University (1965), it had already been perfected and in his ex tempore discourse he was able to produce the same rhythms he achieved in his writing. Perhaps some of his smoothness passed into us by habituation as some of our roughness passed out.

Most of the work we did in class was translation and it was assumed that we would read up on the modern critical literature in our own time. I guess we did, to judge by some of my old essays, and he was of course right to hold that the basic requirement of the classical education was thorough linguistic competence.

I remember in Greek lectures, starting from scratch ignorance and coming across a new important word, we were given a list of all the other passages in the work in hand where that same word recurred.

If they could be jotted down and looked up, they expanded the horizons of the word enormously and added real richness to understanding. We were also taught to appreciate the way ancient writers put their words together to achieve more than the mere literal sum total meaning they bore.

He was highly stimulating. All the Latin poetry I have by heart dates from this period of my life, a sure sign of effective inspiration to learning. Incidentally, I never heard him offer public criticism, only praise and incentive, this commonly taking the form of visions of future academic distinction – the 'when you get to Cambridge' carrot.

That seems odd in retrospect, since he had little time for the Oxbridge myth, but no doubt he considered it a useful ploy to keep pursuing academic excellence. He did not like grading students either, and hated the examination period. But my main impression was a picture of formality, a distant figure endowed with Roman *gravitas*, though one clearly sensed a strong romanticism in his treatment of Horace's farm and Catullus' love.

The Augustani relationship probably began in some way at the morning teas, a feature of the Classics Department under Professor Blaiklock. Classes were timetabled so that senior students and staff could attend these teas, held in Room 004 of the Old Arts Building on Thursdays at 10 a.m.

Closely observed by the framed photographs of previous professors, we would muster, with what home-baking we had, to unlock the biscuit cupboard. There were no tea-making facilities; it was all done at ground-level with an electric jug and power point. Gradually, staff would arrive, the Professor usually last of all from his room across the corridor.

In the heyday of the ritual, the atmosphere was not familiar, unless our family was of another age. The Professor sat at the head of the table in the most impressive chair and was served first. We were overawed, whatever the original intention had been, and were incapable of acting in what I would have called a natural way. The photographs, the seating arrangements, the rectangular table, these served to discourage.

The Professor liked to be the focus of attention and so we spoiled him with his favourite biscuits – a searingly sweet concoction of soft lemon icing and sugary sticky wafers – but we never became familiar, nor did we really get to know him as an individual. We seemed always to be either in Room 004, which served as a student Common Room as well as tearoom, or in 002, where lectures took place.

John Staniland was an Honours student in Blaiklock's last year at the university, an environmentalist and a member of the Augustani. He lived at Waitakere, actively supported the preservation of the Waitakere Ranges from despoliation and welcomed the support Blaiklock gave.

Staniland often wondered just how far Blaiklock would go in protesting over environmental abuses. He was never known to take part in a march of protest. He was very severe in his attitude towards vandals and the angry words he sometimes used and wrote about them, surprised Staniland. On one occasion, with tongue in cheek, Blaiklock had suggested that the death penalty be brought in for vandals.

His love of forests and trees was not just for their beauty but more because of the sense of isolation and security they gave him. He frequently spoke of his Narnia from boyhood days – his 'secret country' among the bays and bush of the

Manukau Harbour and the Waitakeres. Never afraid of being alone for a period, Blaiklock was a loner but not a misanthropist, says Staniland. This comes out quite often in his writings.

Blaiklock could be very sociable and warm-hearted in small groups of people whom he trusted, Staniland continues. But he was insecure in crowds and when travelling by bus, always chose to sit by himself with his own thoughts – and often criticised himself for the habit.

His appreciation of nature was ascetic and scenic rather than strictly biological. He had an intimate knowledge of landscape and his favourite species, but he didn't pretend to be familiar with all species. He was no modern, pure ecologist. He was not afraid to mix the species.

He loved trees and in particular the kauri and wrote of its massive trunks, 'its mighty muscular limbs thrusting strongly skywards'. He found a deep solemnity and encounter with one centuries-old surviving kauri.

Blaiklock had an international appreciation of the natural world, writing about the remaining forests of Lebanon, the beautiful jackarandas of Zimbabwe, the oak forests of Britain. But he was convinced New Zealand was the loveliest of all countries. His greatest joy after travels overseas was in returning to New Zealand, unlocking the door of his Titirangi home – 'and then we were home'.

His ultimate environmentalist fear was the advancing desert, particularly in North and Central Africa, and the drastic resulting changes in climate. These changes had happened before, during and after the days of the Roman Empire. To a far lesser extent and in a different way, he saw similar effects in his own country by the creeping of civilisation into the bush and its accompanying despoliation.

Blaiklock hated goats, which unlike sheep and other animals, can devour all foliage and even start on the soil. Because of their depredations in Asia Minor, he talked of goats as being one of the causes of the fall of the Roman Empire.

John Staniland remarked to Blaiklock that while he agreed goats were destructive, they did have nice faces. Blaiklock replied: 'I can't stand their faces – they remind me of academics.' Staniland was astounded but remembered Blaiklock had never liked the word 'academic'. Its foundation goes back to the very precise members of the Academy in the time of Plato. It meant the closed circle of academics who were 'in the know'. Blaiklock thought of the word in terms of critical people 'the ones who don't really believe anything but think they know everything'. In general terms he was certainly not antagonistic to 'academic man'.

'His well-knit tribe has been my stimulus and my challenge for 40 years,' he could write at the end of his university career.

> I have found a host of friends among them and Christians as sturdy as I have ever hoped to be. Like all other clans of men they have in their number great and small, the valiant and the fearful. They have given me happiness and sometimes suffering. They number among them the truly wise and those who know all the prescribed answers from the first beginnings. There are philosophers, whose very systems would destroy all philosophy, instant theologians on the strength of a specialist degree. They contain the salt of the earth and stereotypes with 'world-view' ready made.

Staniland says not all academics by any means would be in step with Blaiklock for his popularising of the classics as he did so thoroughly through his writings, public speaking and preaching; nor of his criticism of scholars who failed to recognise New Testament documents as authentic historical records of their time.

He had wide knowledge of the New Testament based on history, Greek and Latin – a wider foundation than a great many theologians. He was not one, however, to divide his life into separate compartments – one for conservation, one for Christianity and another for scholarship. Each infiltrated or overlapped the others.

Blaiklock was not averse to introducing humour to illustrate dramatically a point he was seeking to make. On one occasion during the Thursday morning coffee break at the university when Honours students and staff gathered with the Professor once a week, the conversation turned to the reported threat by local council bulldozers, to a group of trees in the Titirangi village centre. Titirangi was the Professor's home district and he was delighted when this subject arose. 'The trees should be preserved, not destroyed,' he claimed. A way to ensure such a result, he proposed, would be if everyone present were to go to Titirangi and to lie down in front of the bulldozers.

A long silence followed as the students waited for his next remark. They knew that when speaking about a subject on which he felt strongly, such as the environment, Blaiklock would often introduce a long pause and follow it by a deliberate 'tongue-in-cheek' remark. They waited for what they knew must come. Recognising it was he who had advocated everyone taking such drastic action, Blaiklock qualified it by saying he would not be able to participate himself as it would be essential for him to survive so as to be able to carry on the fight with his writing of the 'incident' for the newspapers.

During the 1960s, Blaiklock continued writing articles for newspaper and magazines – classical, religious and secular – both for home and overseas publications. By the number of books he authored and had published in that decade, it is amazing he found time to complete them all.

Between 1965–67, A H and A W Reed, of Wellington, published *Ten Pounds an Acre*, *Hills of Home* and *Green Shades*. Bible commentaries published by Pickering and Inglis included Philemon (1964), Romans 12 and 1 Corinthians 13 (1968). The Scripture Union published Blaiklock's studies on Luke (1965) and Romans (1966). Other titles were *Cities of the New Testament* (1965); *No Mists Above* (1966) and *Layman's Answer* (1968).

By the end of 1968, his university career had come to an end, the longest teaching career in the history of the department. He could have retired years sooner but hung on until the last.

His final day was filled with mainly insignificant details. After his last lecture, he stood at the lectern, deep in thought as he watched the students leave. Slowly he followed them out, noticing as he went an inkstain on the sloping floor where a girl had overturned a bottle during the first lecture he had given on the first Monday of March,

1927. That was over forty-one years ago. It seemed only as yesterday and his long career as but a flower that had flourished in full bloom and now had faded.

As he entered his room a girl student came to thank him and say goodbye. It was a deeply emotional occasion for her and she wept; fighting to repress his own emotion, Blaiklock failed and wept with her.

Later he reached in the wardrobe for the gown he had bought from Whipple's in Duncannon Street by Trafalgar Square in London, in 1924, and stood looking at it. It had been with him through so much. It had listened to perhaps one hundred million of his words and it was now telling him it could survive no longer. Tiny slits in its material were now visible.

With a mind that had been fed for a lifetime on literature and the classics, Blaiklock recalled the words of Mark Anthony:

> You all do know this mantle; I remember
> The first time Caesar put it on.
> It was on a summer's evening in his tent,
> The day he overcame the Nervii . . .

Was there an omen here? He folded it up slowly and delicately placed it in his briefcase giving it the full reverence that was its due. He would never wear it again. For future ceremonial occasions, it would be his red doctor's gown.

He unscrewed his nameplate from the door. It was as if, in gathering the last of his personal items, he was about to be put off the street-car of life, on which he had been a passenger for so long. From now on, as it sped on its predetermined way, he would watch it from the sidewalk, rather than as a traveller in the halls of academia.

Before the last day ended, Blaiklock was presented with essays written by eleven former students who had continued in the university classical field. Bruce Harris writes:

> As far as I can remember, the idea of the essays was my own and was a natural one in the light of Blaiklock's long and successful teaching career in the University. We had kept in

touch with virtually all the Auckland Classics graduates who had entered academic life in one way or another. Also, I wanted it known more publicly that, quite irrespective of his Christian activities, he had made his name as a Classicist and that scholars from the department had gone far afield. One curious aspect is that there have been more historians among them than literary people when little serious history was done there. Ted Blaiklock, of course, had a lively historical sense and was an informative and stimulating lecturer on this side but he liked the broad canvas of history and had no taste for the minute scholarship of ancient historians elsewhere.

In 1970, these essays were published by the Auckland University Press and in his introduction to *Auckland Classical Essays, presented to E. M. Blaiklock*, Professor Harris, as its editor, wrote:

> Dr Blaiklock . . . has been a dedicated Classicist who learned his skills chiefly from A.C. Paterson and whose lectures on the Greek tragedians and on Vergil, Horace and Catullus, have perhaps been the most memorable in a very wide range. Without doubt, literature has been his first love, but his interest in Classical history has also been lively and has stimulated many in their formative years. We wish Dr Blaiklock an active and enjoyable retirement.

Those who contributed the essays were: R V Nicholls (Keeper, Department of Antiquities, Fitzwilliam Museum, Cambridge); G L Cawkwell (Fellow of University College, Oxford); W F Richardson (Senior Lecturer in Classics, University of Auckland); L W A Crawley (Associate-Professor of Classics, University of Auckland); R G Mulgan (Professor of Classics, University of Otago); A H McDonald (Fellow of Clare College, Cambridge): D H Kelly (formerly lecturer in Classics, University of Canterbury); R R Dyer (Professor of Classics, Oakland University, Rochester, Michigan); J D Lewis (Senior Lecturer in Classics and Ancient History, University of Western Australia); B F Harris (Senior Lecturer in History (MacQuarie University, Australia); G W Clarke (Professor of Classical Studies, University of Melbourne).

Always conscious of the moods and melancholia from which Blaiklock suffered, Kathleen, as they drove home from an emotional farewell dinner with staff and senior students that evening, sought to lift Blaiklock out of his despondency, 'What you have said over all the years will live on in thousands of students,' she remarked.

An advantage of his retirement, she pointed out, was he would no longer have to undertake the daily drive to and from Titirangi through the increasingly traffic-filled streets. This was becoming a strain. And he sensed that in the university, subtle changes were afoot – 'winds were blowing whose chill I did not like'.

In presenting the book *Auckland Classical Essays* to Blaiklock when it was finally published during his retirement, his associate professor Peter Crawley, at a specially arranged function at the university, spoke of his long association with Blaiklock:

> It is too early for one so close and so intimately involved to make an objective historical assessment of Professor Blaiklock and his tenure of the Chair . . . my own experience can testify to the harmony in the relations between members of the staff and between them and the students which made the Department an object of astonishment to some other sections of the University. It was a hard working but thoroughly pleasant atmosphere in which the spirit was largely due to the Head of Department. He was an energetic champion of both his colleagues and students in contacts outside the Department and a sympathetic and approachable authority within.

# PART FOUR:
# RETIREMENT YEARS

## 10   BLAIKLOCK LEADS TOUR PARTIES

After forty-two years lecturing, counselling of students and administering his own department for twenty-one years, Blaiklock did not find it easy to accept he had finally reached the end of the university road. The next, more relaxed period in his life had, however, been well considered and he had many ideas about how he would occupy his time.

There was the opportunity to spend more time writing, especially on archaeological, geographical, historical and exegetical areas where classical and New Testament studies overlapped. There were translations to do from the New Testament to Thomas à Kempis and Frere Laurent, together with autobiographical writings.

He also looked forward to further special assignments for overseas publishers and to playing his part as a member of the Committee for Bible Translation of the New International Version.

Interspersing all this was to be the care of his section and garden 'when the soil is not revolting mud and one can stand unslithering there to lumber for firewood in my beloved gully full of bush' (*Between the Foothills and the Ridge*, p. 84).

But first there was a leisurely visit overseas to return again to the land of both his and Kathleen's birth and to visit lifelong friends from Kathleen's hometown whom Blaiklock had first come to know during his 'wanderyear' in Great Britain in 1924.

They also visited Africa – visiting the Zambeze river and the Victoria Falls – to capture a little of the enchantment of that vast continent as well as some compassionate understanding of its tormented countries and peoples. Blaiklock spoke to students at Rhodesian and South African universities and what began as a leisurely tour ended a very crowded one.

They returned happy to relax once more in the peace and tranquillity of their Koromiko Road home with its enveloping bush. This was indeed 'home' for them both in a way no other place had been or ever could be. They were content with this as their last overseas trip.

Giving himself to his writing, Blaiklock soon found that the days when his work had been eagerly sought after by overseas book publishers had gone. Following the economic recession in the United States in the early 1970s, plus the increasing popularity of television, the book publishing industry had entered a much more difficult era, particularly for religious titles.

Previously he had had books commissioned by eleven publishers in the United States and Great Britain. He was on Christian name terms with executive editors of most of them and had participated in many of their conferences.

For many years he had been on a retainer fee as a consultant for the Zondervan Publishing House, Grand Rapids, Michigan, USA. Yet despite this background, it was now not easy to get commissions from publishers for the many titles suggested by him. Blaiklock's suggestion for books he could write were numerous but he would not seriously begin one before receiving a commission from a publisher.

In 1978, Ray Richards, a former executive with New Zealand book publishers A H and A W Reed, of Wellington, and now with his own independent literary agency in Auckland, became Blaiklock's literary agent for his secular and New Zealand books. Among others, he was instrumental in getting the Dunmore Press, of Palmerston North, to accept Blaiklock's autobiographical books.

An earlier autobiographical book, *Ten Pounds an Acre*, on Blaiklock's earliest years in New Zealand and his father's unsuccessful attempts to farm the clay soil at Titirangi, had been published in1965 by A H and A W Reed.

Blaiklock's greatest following was in New Zealand where the names of Grammaticus and Blaiklock had long become synonymous to readers of the *New Zealand Herald*. But his massive writing output, plus broadcast programmes and widespread speaking engagements, resulted, to some degree, in his becoming overexposed.

His followers included the many thousands of members of all sections of the Christian church who saw him as a defender of the foundations of Christianity and appreciated his ability to make the faith relevant to life in the twentieth century. But there was a limit to the number of his publications they would buy. For publishers, the choosing of titles that would cover costs had become a very selective process and there were some publishers who saw problems with a writer who had saturated his main market at a time of generally falling book sales.

But difficulties had never before proved insurmountable to Blaiklock and in his retirement years, the number of titles he had published increased from just over sixty to seventy-six.

Some indication of his output of books in his retirement years is seen in this incomplete list with its wide variety of book publishers:

*The Psalms of the Great Rebellion* (Marshall, Morgan & Scott, 1970);
*Apostolic History and the Gospel* (Paternoster Press, 1970);
*Matthew 5 and 6* (Regal Books, California, 1974, 75);
*Epistles of John* (Paternoster & Regal, 1975);
*New Testament Studies* (Markham Press, Texas, 1976);
*First Peter* (Word Books, Texas, 1977);
*The Answers in the Bible* (Hodder & Stoughton, 1978);
*One Vol. Commentary on the New Testament* (Hodder & Stoughton 1978);
*Acts of the Apostles* (Fleming Revell, 1980);
*The Bible and I* (Marshall Morgan & Scott, 1983).

*Autobiographies*
*Between the Valley and the Sea* (Dunmore Press, 1979);
*Kathleen – The Record of a Sorrow* (Hodder & Stoughton 1979);
*Between the Morning and the Afternoon* (Dunmore Press, 1980);
*Between the Foothills and the Ridge* (Dunmore Press, 1981);
*Between the Sunset and the Stars* (Dunmore Press, 1982).

In broadcasting, Blaiklock's contributions were not as prolific as in his writing but over the years beginning in 1935, they were substantial. They included historical, archaeological and reflective talks, Jim Henderson's Open Country, many *Faith for Today* series, numerous Church broadcasts, book reviews and interviews and editorials for the *Listener*. The first of his autobiographical books written in his retirement, *Between the Valley and the Sea*, was broadcast as a ten-part series for the 10.30 p.m. National Programme from 1 June 1981.

Blaiklock's radio talks gained him a following right throughout the country and many favourable reviews and comments in newspapers. Clippings of favourable comments of his writings and radio talks were kept but unfortunately practically all of these were undated.

It is remarkable that a man with such a mind for detail in everything else, should ignore dates in items which affected his own work. He was not a great letter writer himself but in some of those he wrote by his own hand, the same omission occurs. The following is one such undated clipping of a newspaper writer's comment on one of his radio talks, 'The World to which Christ Came':

> It is a subject before which a lesser man might quail. But the erudite Professor Blaiklock had plunged in and given us a most human commentary about human beings so like ourselves that immediately we begin to understand and to see Palestine as it was nearly 2000 years ago. His talk brought to life most vividly the Sadducees and Pharisees, sects of the Jewish church of Christ's day. No shadowy figures half understood but now compellingly third-dimensional. This is the stuff of radio without a doubt; to bring such historical but easily understood and remembered material to the microphone. I would say that Professor Blaiklock does more by himself and his choice of words than possibly even a wide-screen could. Arguable perhaps, but the power of a simple description to summon up the swelling scene is not to be denied. The rest is over to the listener. And that, surely, was all that Shakespeare asked in his Chorus to *Henry V*.

Among his papers was also found a comment on Radio New Zealand notepaper in the handwriting of a producer of the corporation's *Faith for Today* series – also undated and whose signature it is impossible to decipher. As it is nevertheless clearly a genuine comment, it is reprinted as another example of his outstanding gift of communication whether with students in lectures, readers of his books, listeners to his radio talks or viewers on his television series:

> You are the undisputed champion among our contributors at using words. Your evocative description of the memorial service at Chunuk Bair, for example, created an effect which is, quite simply, not approached by anyone else. Letters from listeners confirm this; there were numerous requests for scripts. One listener said: 'I need to read them again because when I listened I became caught up in simply listening to the words.' Style, approach, vocabulary – each is very much your own. The subject matter makes greater demands on the listeners than do many that we broadcast and yet we find this to be one of the reasons for their popularity. Listeners are introduced to ideas, writings and philosophies which are new to them; but the underlying message never fails to come through.

While imagining that the rest of his retirement years would be spent in writing, preaching and occasional visits overseas, Blaiklock, in 1972, was asked to lead groups of Christians as tour parties to the Middle East, Europe and the United States. In this decade, he was to lead seven such tour parties.

George Bremner had been leader of the Crusader Group at Mt Albert Grammar School during the years when both Peter and David were pupils there. He had thus developed a friendship with the family and had often consulted Blaiklock on questions of the early Christian documents and their reliability.

In 1969, Bremner organised a party, of six Christians under the name Evangelical Travel Association, for a round-the-world trip. This was undertaken as an exploratory one to see if world tours of Christians in one group were feasible. He had noticed on ordinary commercial tours that matters of particular interest to Christians were largely ignored. In

1971 a second such world tour was arranged and this convinced George his idea was a practical one.

He first approached Blaiklock for advice on details of an itinerary he had plotted for a tour for Christians to include Middle East countries. During the conversation he asked Blaiklock if he would be interested in leading such a tour party. He was delighted. 'I thought my travelling days were done,' he said.

Blaiklock made changes to the itinerary, agreed to lead the 1972 tour and also to his name being used to promote it. There were forty-eight on the first tour. Other tours followed in 1974, 1975, 1977, 1979, 1980 and 1981. Blaiklock wrote later about the tours as follows:

> I was asked to lead travel parties to the dozen lands I knew. It was to fill the years for us. We led archaeological parties to Israel, Turkey, Greece, Crete and the Aegean islands, to Italy, Switzerland, France and Britain wherever Rome had trod or Greece had penetrated from Troy to Carlisle, Bath to Beersheba. We have built tours round English history, British archaeology and the story of America. It has been immensely fulfilling and a great challenge to weld groups of New Zealanders and Australians into teams of friends, eager always to unite and talk.
>
> (*Between the Foothills and the Ridge*, p. 88)

Blaiklock's job on the tour was to give members of the party the benefit of his knowledge of the history and historical figures of the places visited. Local guides were also used and these Blaiklock worked with closely.

On each bush trip he ensured the front seat was his. It gave him access to the microphone. Following the local guide announcing where the next trip was taking them, Blaiklock would then speak, making the place come alive with his recalling of its history and local colour.

Reuben Ben Dori, was the proprietor of Galilee Tours with whom Gateway Travel worked on their tours to the Middle East. (George Bremner had by this time succeeded in securing an International Air Travel Association agency under which he changed the name of his organisation, the Evangelical Travel Association, to Gateway Travel.) When

Ben Dori learned of Blaiklock's part in a forthcoming tour, he sought the highest academically qualified guide he could find to work with him. The guide, Yoram, was a fluent speaker of French, Hebrew, English and Italian. He had grave misgivings when he learnt he was to share the tour commentaries with a professor and classical scholar.

When the party arrived in Israel, however, Blaiklock quickly won the confidence of Yoram, who in no time became relaxed enough to confide in him of his earlier misapprehensions. These were days in which Israel was being attacked by raids from Arab territory. Blaiklock was comforted to notice that on their travels by bus through Israel, Yoram (who was also an officer in the Israeli army) carried a sub-machine gun with him, having it lying on the floor of the bus within handy reach.

Before the start of the 1975 tour, which was majoring on Great Britain, Blaiklock was to address the tour party and friends at an evening meeting of about 200 in the Presbyterian Church hall in Khyber Pass, Auckland.

It was timed to start at 7.30 p.m. At 7.25, as Bremner arranged the seating and table for the speaker, Blaiklock came hurrying down the aisle. Looking somewhat agitated (quite unusual for him before addressing a meeting), Blaiklock said: 'George, whatever am I to talk to them about?' Taken back, Bremner said that anything about Britain and its history would do. After being briefly introduced, Blaiklock spoke without notes for an hour and ten minutes. He talked of the overlapping of cultures in Britain's past, the intermingling of peoples from practically every other European country and the affect of this in the emergence of the Anglo-Saxon. He quoted, without a reference to notes, from Shakespeare and Longfellow. Throughout he held his audience spellbound. As he concluded, the audience spontaneously rose to its feet as one and applauded vigorously.

As tour party leader, Blaiklock was not called on to manage matters of travel and the itinerary. A business manager was appointed for every trip just for this purpose. Often it was someone from Blaiklock's own family. His son David went on four of the trips as manager. For him and other members of the family including grandchildren, the trips were unforgettable experiences, as they were for tour party members also:

> Dad's contribution of rare sensitivity and eloquence left an indelible impression on us all. Whether in the middle of the Sea of Galilee, on top of Masada or at the Garden Tomb in Jerusalem at 6 a.m., he always said just the right words with the right emphases.
> 
> He was at his happiest and best when we visited old theatres such as Epidauras and Delphi in Greece and Ephesus in Turkey. In these places with their extraordinary acoustics, he loved to give an oration in the ancient tongue. In Ephesus he gave the town clerk's speech from Acts 19 when he addressed the crowd who were then mobbing Paul. Tourists other than those with our own party would always stop, listen and applaud generously whether English, French or Germans. He always had a commanding presence and in these circumstances he carried it off magnificently.

Norma Warwick, who organised his Australian visits, writes of several of the tour parties of which she was a member:

> The countries visited included Hong Kong, Singapore, Israel, Turkey, Greece and the Greek Islands, Italy, Austria, Switzerland, Germany, the Netherlands, France, Britain, Canada and the United States (he loved Disneyland). Not every country was visited on every trip.
> 
> It was profoundly moving to share his vast knowledge and to see these countries, particularly Israel, through his eyes. Bible stories came to vivid life as famous places were visited: Mt Carmel, Caesarea Philippi, Ashkelon, Jericho and many others. Prof. was impatient of the monuments at some of the places of sacred memory. 'How typical of man,' he would say, 'to put something gaudy on a place where God wanted to teach a simple truth'. Perhaps this was one of the reasons why he preferred to accept the beautiful Garden Tomb with its skull-like hill nearby as the site of the Lord's death and burial rather than the Church of the Holy Sepulchre. His graphic description of events gripped the mind at these places as well as at the Pavement, the Garden of Gethsemane and the Mount of Olives; while to share in a simple Sunday service under the

olive trees on the Emmaus road was an experience never to be forgotten.

The earthly ministry of the Lord took on a new meaning in Galilee when Prof. spoke on the Beatitudes as the moonlight shimmered on the waters of the lake, or told stories from the Gospels at Capernaum, Cana and Nazareth, or on the Lake itself as the water quietly lapped the sides of the boat. In Turkey the sites of most of the seven churches of Asia Minor referred to in Revelation were visited, with fresh thoughts on each offered from Prof.'s imaginative mind. To be at Troy brought the story of Ulysses to life, while on Gallipoli at Easter, a message on sacrifice made an indelible impression. Prof. always maintained that without a knowledge of the past we could not understand the present. He illustrated this graphically as he led his parties through Greece ((birthplace of our democracy) and Italy, drawing on his wealth of knowledge of classical history, literature, the Bible and its archaeology.

To be in Britain with Prof. – England's green and pleasant land, the hills and valleys of Wales, the highlands and lochs of Scotland – was an enviable experience. The endless lines of poetry stored in his memory were shared with his companions in the Lake Country or at Hadrian's Wall, or wherever a scene evoked a memory. Being on tour with him was, to use his own words, 'a delight which has been like a late lark singing'.

So unique an experience was it for most that on their return home, reunions of tour parties became commonplace. The 1975 group, as just one example, held an annual reunion for ten consecutive years, some members coming to Auckland for the earlier ones from as far away as the South Island, across the Tasman and even from Perth, Western Australia.

In 1971 Blaiklock became president of the Baptist Union of New Zealand, the same year in which he was named one of the one hundred makers of Auckland in a special *New Zealand Herald* centennial (1871–1971) poll of readers and, in 1974 he was awarded the OBE (Order of the British Empire) in the Queen's birthday honours list for his 'services to scholarship and the community'.

In appointing him to its highest office, the Baptist Union felt it should honour him for his stature in the community, fame abroad and his commitment to the local church. The honour was not conferred on him because of any specific contributions he had made to the denomination's boards and committees, from which he had withdrawn in the 1940s.

Blaiklock had always been loyal to his local Baptist church. This was the Baptist Tabernacle, where he and Kathleen had been married, and from where they transferred to Mt Albert Baptist Church in 1940, following a major split in the Tabernacle congregation, when a majority transferred to suburban churches. But Blaiklock was never a 'narrow' member of the Baptist denomination. He showed little respect for ecclesiastical machinery and a healthy disrespect for some clergy.

Dr Bob Thompson, formerly principal of the Baptist Theological College, believes the word 'great' may be truly ascribed to Blaiklock:

> In the circles in which I have moved in a dozen trips around the world, Blaiklock was, through his writings or visits, New Zealand's best known Christian. Any anthology of the 100 great New Zealanders would have to include his name.
>
> For most people he was kindly, helpful and fair but for some people, some of the time, he was less than fully just, although by his own standards he had reason enough for acting the way he did.
>
> Wise? Yes, if by wisdom we mean 'the final and embracing objective . . . the essential ingredient of understanding distilled from knowledge, the cream and essence of things learned . . .' to use phrases from one of his latest radio broadcasts – *The Path to Understanding*. Perhaps even wisest, if by that one means hearing the centuries rather than the decades and plotting our position today in relation to all human thought. What he gave me was this sense of eternity within time and abiding values among the passing.

In his presidential address to the eighty-eighth assembly of the Baptist Union in Dunedin, Blaiklock expressed criticism of

> the anxious theologians who have fallen into a lamentable scramble to adjust to a passing fashion of thought.
>
> The reason for this may have something to do with a few

catch-cries, those ancient substitutes for reason. The first century had the same malady.

Many modern protagonists allegedly speak the language of today but in fact, often end in speaking no intellectual language at all, if communication, honest and clear is the criterion of speech. The tragedy is the easy victory this small band of iconoclasts, including Tillich, Bultmann and John Robinson (proponents of the 'New Theology'), have won over churchmen of feeble faith.

Surely it is time to have done with the delusions of the 1960s. There is a battle ahead, if we take up the old imagery of Christian soldiering. Linked together as we face the fight are the quality of our belief, the quality of our living and the quality of our lives.

The world at large, which looks with tolerant contempt on the compromising, agnostic churchman, holds some respect for the Christian who stands uncompromisingly for what he believes to be true, for what he proclaims to be good and who fearlessly preaches it and tangles with life.

It matters supremely what we believe and specially what kind of person we believe in. Underpinning all our living, giving point, purpose and reality to our preaching, is the quality of our belief. Uncertainty is communicable.

We have a proclamation to make to this decade and this century. We must charge our spokesman to deliver it with authority and conviction. We must all demonstrate there is one happy breed who can find zest for life, health of mind and creativity in self-control, chastity and the age-old values of Christianity. Only thus shall we permeate society and win a distracted mankind to Christ.

Blaiklock also spoke frequently to civic and cultural groups as he travelled throughout the country visiting Baptist churches in his year as president.

In Palmerston North he opened the Third National Computer Conference, linking the modern computer to St John's vision of the beast as described in the book of Revelation. The beast rose out of the sea and laid hold of society, he said. All received a mark on their right hands and on their foreheads that no man might buy or sell save he who had the mark of the beast or the number of his name.

Rome was not the first tyranny the world had known and St John's protest was not the first man had raised against an authority which sought to depersonalise him, give him a number, make him a cog in some manipulated machine and eliminate the non-conforming few.

Man feared what he failed to understand. He was conscious of something emerging greater than himself. There were tribesmen who never told their names because to know a name meant power over its bearer. Hence the well-known uneasiness over the storing of information (beneficial though that information could be), because of fear of its misuse and anger over privacy invaded.

What man truly feared was man and in his heart every person was aware that no invention in history had escaped misuse from the bow and arrow to nuclear power. Blaiklock continued:

> I fear the computer could harm mankind's capacity to learn and to know. We lay waste our powers when we fail to use them.
>
> In moments of pessimism one could imagine the society of H. G. Wells' time-machine coming to reality with those who command machines ruling a mindless world. It is but a small step from that point to abandoning the glory of our humanity and worshipping the idol, the things our own hands have made. Here are dangers real enough in your profession and its tools.
>
> Security, liberty, privacy are part of our heritage and the common man is right to fear for the safety of that which, after all, is a fragile growth, too often trodden down in our own times by the booted heel of authority. A faith in robots can make robots of those who exercise that faith; and humanity, too reliant on its tools, can be dehumanised by them.
>
> What then is the remedy? First to hold fast to the noblest view of man. It is no use establishing a 'code of ethics' for the use of computers. For codes, as our age shows too well, in too many spheres, can be ridiculed, changed, abandoned. There are no morals in a machine; they can exist, where they do exist, only in the machinist. Hence the point I make. Man's safety lies in man's moral responsibility and that responsibility derives from man's view of himself.
>
> If man looks upon himself as an animal, he will behave like

one. Viewed merely as a machine or animal or insect, man is ill-equipped. It is only an extraordinary 'something else' which makes him different from all else.

To pupils of the Auckland Girls' Grammar School at their annual prize-giving, he spoke of scientific achievement:

> To explore the back of the moon and penetrate deep space is an empty achievement if no wonder lights the task, if new experience means nothing in terms of the spirit.
> The spirit of man would be the poorer if the music of the spheres were lost in facts about the spheres; if the first men to explore the spheres were tight-lipped robots, unable to wonder, to dream or know the thrill of poetry, or more, know humility.
> Let us hold fast to the world of wonder, beauty, reverence. If in history you have never wondered at the ancient heroisms and old endeavours of man, if in science you have never stood in awe at the amazing spectacles of nature, if the symmetry and order which make the beauty of mathematical truth have never stirred humble and solemn thoughts, you remain uneducated, a mere mechanical brain wired to regurgitate information stacked cunningly within.

Speaking to Rotarians in Tauranga, Blaiklock stressed there was a moral law in history which could not be broken: 'You cannot get more out of life than you put into it.'

Speaking on Christian education to the Middleton Grange School in Christchurch, Blaiklock said an education system which did not use the Bible was a system which had lost a great deal of value:

> The Bible – that marvellous compendium of human experience – which has shaped everything worthwhile in the modern world, is the book society will lose at its peril. A Christian education takes into account the threefold nature of man – body, soul and spirit. Education today emphasizes science. Science, or knowledge, is necessary but it should not become the master.
> Discipline is necessary to learning and a Christian should include discipline, instead of the prevalent idea that a child

should not be compelled to do anything he did not want to.

Man has to decide what constitutes his happiness. If it is material things, then man is doomed by the year 2000, if not earlier.

This life is a reflection of another life – a life of higher quality. We should implant the idea of this life in our children as part of their education.

Blaiklock gave his wholehearted support to organisations such as the Scripture Union and the Bible Societies which propagated the Bible as authoritative, reliable and relevant for today. As president of the Bible Society of New Zealand, he gave the second Olivier Beguin Memorial Lecture in 1975 in many centres in New Zealand and Australia. Sponsored by the Bible Society, the lecture was a tribute to a former secretary of the United Bible Societies from 1949–72.

Extracts from his address 'The Authority and Relevance of the Bible in the Modern World,' were quoted in a number of secular and church papers. After reading his address, Rev B E Hibbert, editor of the *New Zealand Baptist*, commented as follows:

> It is an impressive utterance on a grand theme. But as with everything Professor Blaiklock writes, it is the style and craftsmanship, evident in every line, which first catches the attention and then reinforces the argument being developed. Every word seems to be carefully selected, every sentence honed to a point of precision with the end result a blend of poetry and logic rarely achieved except by masters of the art.

He then quoted Blaiklock's concluding paragraph:

> Can this century of tyrannies avoid the evil thing which rises out of the sea to put a mark on head and hand and deny food and work to those who will not sell their souls? Can this day fail to shudder at the bright and poisoned thing which falls death-laden into the sea and horsemen which ride forth to kill and starve and take the price of food beyond the poor man's buying? And must we not long for the end of tears, for some rich and new Jerusalem beside an unpolluted river?'

Blaiklock's regular weekly Grammaticus articles for the *New Zealand Herald* were not forgotten. They were continued without fail until he could write no more. A condensed version of one such article appearing at this time, entitled 'Campaign for Silence', is as follows:

> The sounds of trees, of wind and water seldom harm us, even when they roar and strive. Most sounds of Nature are gentle, low, mingled with the total of our senses. Noise is man's own demonic invention. Think of the scream of the jet engine, the rattle of the helicopter, the clatter of a dozen typewriters, of all most evil intrusions on the air, the fearsome cacophony of amplified modern music.
>
> And this horror can pursue us down the street from the transistor of some poor youth afraid to be alone, or to the proper haunts of quietness in the bush or by the sea where the same addicts must carry the tools of their affliction and impose it like a virus on the rest.
>
> One of the thoughts of that sensitive being Blaise Pascal is a confession that he found 'the eternal silence of infinite space' terrifying. Wordsworth spoke of our 'noisy years' as but a few moments' interruption in the eternal silence. Carlyle, twice according to the dictionary, attaches silence to eternity and Tennyson makes his valiant Ulysses fight to snatch another hour 'from that eternal silence'.
>
> In a quiet street near the college where I lodged (in London), I met a handful of youths. In those days it was no occasion for fear as it would be today. But it was deathly silent. The boys themselves were not speaking until one of them, unable to endure the stillness, stood, threw back his head and howled like a wolf at the stars. The silence had frightened him, not with Pascal's sense of littleness and awe, but in sheer pain at being alone with his thoughts.
>
> That is how the growing noise of the world is altering the nature of man. Quietness leaves us alone with the content of our minds. We think, and to the simplest minds come thoughts of beauty; conscience has time to work, to confront us with our manner of living, to sort out false values and to stir that salutary discontent which makes a better person of a human being. I am sure that silence heals, that noise, forever surrounding us, produces that mad desire to escape, which is part of a 'nervous breakdown'.
>
> We must have done with pollution. We must treasure and

extend our zones of silence in wilderness and even in our cities. We must have done with the yelling madness of collective celebration audible beyond the physical confines of those in thrall to it. We must forbid radios in public and have done with piped noise in all buildings. Noisy 'parties' must be put down. You extend the list. It is time for an uprising.

Another newspaper clipping from a satisfied Grammaticus reader (again undated), was among those kept by Blaiklock in his untidy file of clippings:

Grammaticus has the enviable gift of being able to say things what others feel is right but cannot say for the simple reason they lack his knowledge of the apt word and allusion and his talent for writing with grammatic fluency and clarity.

But perhaps another reason is that he does not seek in the garbage tins of humanity and, under the label of realism, to devote himself to a discussion of the sordid sides of life which so many writers today seem to imagine is typical of the whole of life. Grammaticus finds his subjects simply by stepping outside his front or back door. He finds beauty in normal, everyday things – which his readers are convinced are much more common, thank goodness, than the abnormal. And if he has any complaints, they are against the soulless clods who destroy what is naturally beautiful, or deprive natural man of his natural rights. Long may he write! – SUBSCRIBER, New Plymouth.

The Augustani continued to meet together every year. Dr Vivienne Gray had missed several of the earlier meetings while she had been overseas but rejoined them again on her return. She writes:

When I returned, the old formality still persisted. But now Blaiklock kissed us when we met and we exchanged phone calls.

Many of us enjoyed alcohol but we were unwilling to drink it openly at these meetings because we knew the Professor did not drink and had strong principles about it. I now find such deference very odd but it did happen and has its explanation in the fact that these meetings were, at the beginning, continuations of the old morning teas.

In these earlier meetings, the Professor was the centre and heart of the business; it was done for him. This was not his fault – at that stage he may indeed have wanted our fellowship to become more familiar – but we were incapable of breaking too quickly from the mould. In the end he did not turn a hair when the flagon was introduced, and gradually, the fellowship mellowed. I was bound to have a lot to discuss with him because of our common interest in University teaching and the Classics Department. Others found interest with him in religion or Nature or school teaching.

In his retirement years he was worried about the new direction the Classics Department had taken, developing Ancient History, so he said, at the expense of languages. He was not right but I could never convince him otherwise. Certainly, more students were taking Greek language than in his day and there were many more MA Greek candidates than I ever remember. There was a reduction in the numbers taking Latin 1, beginning in 1970, but it was due to the decline of Latin in the schools and other factors beyond our control rather than to any neglect of languages on our part. But I never did convince him that we were doing all we could to foster the languages. Sometimes I suspect that he actually preferred to believe that things were better managed in his day; but management was not really the issue.

Arrangements for Blaiklock's speaking engagements did not always go according to plan. In 1975, the year in which he retired as president of the Bible College of New Zealand, he was scheduled to give the address at the college's annual graduation service.

In arranging the end-of-year function, the college principal, David Stewart, had agreed to twenty minutes being set aside for a drama production by students. While studying for their examinations, the students did not leave themselves enough time for thorough preparation of their drama production. On the night of the graduation service they took one hour to complete it instead of the allotted twenty minutes. Blaiklock had been timed to give the graduation address beginning shortly after 8.30 p.m. It was 9.30 p.m. before he arose to speak.

Stewart's recollection is vivid:

> He was really upset. I don't think he ever quite forgave us. He didn't express his disapproval in the Auckland Town Hall but one could cut the air with a knife afterwards.
>
> He was critical of the whole play and this was a bit unfair. I had encouraged it because I considered it was something creative for the graduation. I thought the students did it very well although they took three times longer than they should. He was never appreciative of anything we did in the creative ministries.

According to Stewart, Blaiklock also had reservations about the charismatic movement. He was very suspicious of it. He saw it as being anti-intellectual. Speaking in tongues was almost an anathema to him.

The issue came to a head in Blaiklock's last year as president. The principal reported that only about six or ten of the students were of the 'difficult' charismatic type. After a board discussion, Stewart was asked to look into the matter further and report back.

The next year Stewart circulated a questionnaire to all students asking their church affiliation, were they 'charismatic' Christians, had they spoken in tongues and if so, were they continuing to use the tongues experience in their personal devotions?

Neither the principal nor the board were prepared for the results of the questionnaire. About forty percent of the student body had had a tongues experience! 'I realised I had been unfair in my earlier assessment of the students,' said Stewart. 'I had judged all charismatic people on this small "difficult" group. The questionnaire came as a shock. It was quite a revelation.'

The board discussed it at length over several months. Stewart urged that with so many charismatic students, the college had to be open about the issue and encourage all students: 'In my report I recommended that for those who had been helped by a "baptism of the Spirit" experience or by speaking in tongues, we should thank God and urge them to go on allowing the Holy Spirit to fill their lives.'

It was decided to allow David Stewart's report to 'lie on

the table' for three months. Board members were invited to pray about the report and to submit their comments on it in writing. Three members wrote negatively. Stewart replied to their comments. The question was then again referred to a later meeting. When this took place, the three members who had opposed the principal's report, individually reaffirmed their personal opposing views, but said they believed the college should adopt the policy as outlined in the report of the principal.

When the issue was finally resolved in this way, Blaiklock himself acknowledged it as being the correct one for the college. He even spoke of the decision as a model for other groups and churches to follow.

Although he was never free of reservations about charismatic Christians, he enjoyed preaching in a number of mainline denominational churches where the movement flourished and where he welcomed the warm response by members to his messages. This also applied to the Titirangi Presbyterian Church where he had preached regularly for over fifty years and of which he considered himself a part, second only to his own Mt Albert Baptist Church.

There was another matter just ahead of him that would make his attitude to the anti-intellectualism of charismatics, of no consequence to him. Kathleen's life was nearing its end. Blaiklock was to become emotionally drained to the depths as he watched her slowly die and, in her passing, to face the greatest personal crisis of his life.

# 11   KATHLEEN DIES

The fourth overseas travel tour which Blaiklock led for Gateway Travel was to leave Auckland and Sydney on 1 May 1977 for Hong Kong, Greece, Turkey, the Aegean Islands, Israel and Switzerland plus two weeks in Britain, on to Los Angeles and Honolulu, returning home on 14 June. It was the last one Kathleen was to take.

Early in February of that year Kathleen found she was having difficulty putting words in their right order in her speech. 'I am confusing my words,' she said to Blaiklock. 'I think I must have had a slight stroke.'

This happened with the next round-the-world trip just weeks away. They decided to go ahead, hoping the travel would result in an improvement in Kathleen's health. Kathleen travelled as usual as a member of the party, saying little. Blaiklock's concern for her increased as the tour progressed.

During a visit to Galilee as he sat under a magnolia, he heard someone distantly reading the sermon on the mount. As the boy's voice read on, Blaiklock thought of the literal rendering: 'Keep on praying, keep on asking . . .' As he spent time alone he became convinced God was promising him Kathleen would get better.

By August, Blaiklock's optimism and faith were wavering. Kathleen had not improved. They visited a neurologist. It was not a stroke Kathleen was suffering from but a brain tumour, he informed Blaiklock. 'Then must I watch her slowly die?' Blaiklock exclaimed in anguish. There was no answer but the silence of the neurologist rang more loudly through his whole being than any words could have done.

To a friend in England, Blaiklock wrote at that time:

> The one who has talked to me, advised and admonished me for 49 years of married life lives with undamaged intelligence so far, behind a wall of frustrating silence. We cannot even pray together, though she understands my words. The skies may grow darker yet. I have cancelled all engagements but find I can still write and I find some relief in so doing.
>
> (*Kathleen*, foreword, p. 8)

By the end of November it was decided Kathleen needed more help than Blaiklock could give. Her speech was now completely gone and her right leg no longer held her. Her two daughters-in-law came for her on 29 November. Marjorie, wife of son David and herself a nursing sister, was to take care of her in their home.

Solemnly Blaiklock watched Kathleen as she was helped to the car from her home, right foot lifted on Marjorie's left and assisted also by Jean, Peter's wife. Blaiklock followed behind driving himself the seven miles to David and Marjorie's home. That night he returned alone to 47 Koromiko Road.

Later Kathleen went into hospital. Granddaughter Alison was a senior student at the Auckland Medical Hospital across the road from the Auckland Hospital in Grafton. She visited Kathleen as often as possible.

On 8 February Kathleen was failing. Blaiklock and Alison, after sitting beside the still peaceful form of Kathleen, decided to have lunch together. When they left, Kathleen was deeply comatose but visibly alive. As they were returning to her room about one o'clock, a young doctor hurried forward: 'Professor, your wife passed away seven minutes ago.' Blaiklock and Alison knelt together in prayer by her lifeless form. Then Alison went to the telephone. Blaiklock felt Kathleen's brow grow chill beneath his hand and kissed her cold, pale lips. Nearly fifty years of married life had ended. Blaiklock was never to be the same again.

Two years earlier when Blaiklock and Kathleen had been driving home after a happy day's outing, they had discussed the inevitability of one outliving the other. Blaiklock expressed the hope that Kathleen would be taken first and thus spared the pain of separation. 'That's real love,' Kathleen had rejoined. Now that time had arrived. Blaiklock had his wish. But he was totally unprepared for the overwhelming grief that ensued – a grief that ebbed and flowed on his emotions strongly at first but always continued throughout his remaining days.

In the mundane things he found it difficult to cope – housekeeping, meals, washing, ironing and particularly the packing of his bags before a local or overseas trip. These things Kathleen had always attended to thoroughly and expertly.

She had in fact subjugated her whole life to serving Blaiklock. It was to her a calling from God. Her contribution to his life was immeasurable. On two occasions following her death, Blaiklock wrote of her as follows:

> I cannot measure the gratitude I have for all Kathleen brought to me with her qualities of heart and mind . . . It is difficult to describe such friendship. It goes deeper than all words can say . . . she polished and refined me, quenched with gentleness much that was ill . . . I cannot begin to grasp what life might have been had it not been for Kathleen. I find myself pausing like a Jewish scribe, before I write that name . . .
> (*Between the Foothills and the Ridge*, p. 75)
> She gave me much that I would never have elsewhere found, a sensitivity to others' feelings, a steadying hand on hot reactions, a passion for order, forethought and efficiency.
> (*Kathleen*, p. 62)

David speaks of his mother as follows:

> She wrote twice to me every week when I was a medical student at Dunedin. Her effect on my life was as a quiet background of encouragement. She obviously supplied the same role for Dad as for me, because by nature he had melancholic tendencies – the negative side of his sensitive nature.
>   Although we knew they had a very deep love for each other, we did not realise just how much he needed her until her death. Dad was devastated by the loss and never really recovered in the six years he had left although the last two years seemed to those close to him, easier for him.

I personally found his grief overwhelming and difficult to come to terms with for some time during which he turned to me and Peter for constant support. An eminent visiting physician recently stated that an event such as severe grief could so shatter the body's immune system that a malignancy could result. [Blaiklock died just five years eight months after Kathleen, from cancer! (T.S.)]

Warnock Watson recalls one occasion when Blaiklock and Kathleen came to dinner. They were all chatting together in the lounge after the meal when Blaiklock put his hand in his pocket, apparently to find a handkerchief but withdrew it empty. While the conversation continued, Kathleen quietly opened her bag, withdrew a handkerchief and slipped it to him. 'There was a wonderful empathy between them,' Watson remarked.

Rev J Oswald Sanders, lecturer at the Bible College from its founding days by Joseph Kemp and its principal when the latter died (Sanders later became a missionary leader, Bible teacher and author), was also a close friend of the Blaiklocks throughout their lives. In an article on Kathleen for the *Reaper* (official organ of the Bible College), Sanders quoted a portion of the oration Wendel Phillips gave at the funeral of John Brown: 'Some people struggle into obscurity while others forget themselves into immortality.' This, he wrote, was Kathleen. She was just as self-forgetful.

She absolutely gave herself for him, in fact too much so. Blaiklock never really recovered from his loss but was better towards the end. He suffered inwardly terribly through those early days of Kathleen's going, far more than people realise. I had been through it twice but I couldn't help him. He literally refused to be comforted. A verse from the Psalms that applied to him was: 'My soul refused to be comforted'. He wanted to hug his sorrow.

He told me that while on tour in Israel when Kathleen's tumour was thought to be only a slight stroke, he went into the hills of Galilee alone to spend time with the Lord. He came away sure God had spoken to him that Kathleen would get better. 'And then she died,' he said. 'How can I ever again know when God is speaking to me?'

A former principal of the Auckland Technical Institute and president of the Bible College following Blaiklock's retirement, Ivan Moses was another close friend of the Blaiklocks. He was sympathetic to Blaiklock in his deep grief and they talked together about it at length. Moses believed some of the things that tortured him in his post-Kathleen days sprung strangely from the attributes and abilities that had made him what he was.

There was his unique memory by which he could repeat a poem through after reading it only once; his vast and detailed knowledge of history and historical figures of every age, illustrations which he used to encourage, enlighten and inspire others in four continents. There was also his certainty about the New Testament documents, their reliability and their accounts of the resurrection of Jesus Christ as the only rational explanation of the events of those days; in so many ways on so many occasions he had spoken and written about the sure foundations of the Christian faith. Now in his own deepest need, he felt an enemy was throwing them all back at him, saying: 'Yes, you've all the answers; here are your very own words, but they are not working for you, are they?'

There was his deep love for Kathleen and their nearly fifty years of an intensely satisfying marriage. It was not easy for so sensitive a romantic to adjust to life without her, nor to know how to cope with the many memories of her that continued daily to flood his mind: 'Today the anniversary of her passing; tomorrow the full year . . . exactly five years ago she appeared on the terrace in front of the dining room and begged me to be careful . . .'

The carpets in the house remind him they had been chosen by her, as do the shrubs in the garden. In searching through a drawer he finds a prayer in Kathleen's handwriting and dwells on it. It is for 'lonely people, especially those who come home to an empty house, stand at the door, hesitant and afraid to open . . .' Had Kathleen placed it there deliberately?

His son's birthday recalls the long hours of Kathleen's agony in labour . . . leading a tour party around the world he does what he has to; talks of a thousand things from the front of the bus, makes conversation at the meal table which others say is stimulating. But when he returns to his room alone at night and sees again the suitcase that was hers and which he deliberately chose to take with him, his grief takes over. He climbs into bed, empty, desolate and unable to restrain the sobs because Kathleen is no longer with him.

Dean Rymer and Mrs Rymer often went to Titirangi for meals with Blaiklock and Kathleen. As soon as Kathleen was admitted to hospital the Dean was advised and visited both of them.

'Kathleen couldn't talk but I could talk to her. She was a strong woman and she could understand what I was saying, I am sure,' the Dean says.

> What I realised at that time was that Blaiklock would never have been who he was if she had not been his support. She was more than just his wife; she was his total supporting strength and I had never before noticed it. She was always in the background. It was where she wanted to be.
>
> The day she died I visited her while Blaiklock and Alison went to have a meal in the Domain. I was the last person to see her alive. There was a flicker of recognition and I prayed with her. I realised then, how strong a woman she was. There was no way her faith was weakened nor any sign of a loss of it with the approach of death.

Dean Rymer and Sir Martin Sullivan pressed on Blaiklock the need for a book from him on the triumph of a Christian passing through the death experience of a loved one. He was hesitant. There was nothing victorious about his Christian experience since Kathleen's death, he reasoned. If he wrote anything, it would have to be an honest account of his grief and despair. He knew that was not what others wanted. But they persisted and Blaiklock gave in. It was certainly not what was expected.

Then religious publishing director of Hodder and Stoughton, London, Edward England, wrote in his foreward to *Kathleen*, as follows:

> It was only last summer I was privileged to visit his home in Titirangi. Six months earlier his wife had died. I understood his

agony for a few years before I had lost my own dear partner. Suddenly I saw him no longer as the distinguished former Professor of Classics in the University of Auckland, the author of numerous books in the spheres of New Testament studies and Greek classical drama . . . He now belonged to the fellowship of those who know the most intense of personal bereavements.

When he first shared these pages with me I knew it was almost too personal to publish and to do so may be indulgence. But my request was based on a belief that it may meet some needs more than most 'books of comfort' do.

Criticism of the book *Kathleen* was instant. It came from those who knew him as the Professor of Classics, the master of the apt phrase, the expert par excellence in the use of the English language. They were disappointed they could no longer find the free-flowing pen backed by the brilliant mind in any page of *Kathleen*. Instead the book revealed the pen of an old man in the slough of despondency and the grip of grieving despair.

Those who had urged on Blaiklock the task of writing *Kathleen* were disappointed. Lady Elizabeth Sullivan, echoed the views, no doubt, of more than those of her late husband when she commented: 'This book should never have been published.'

Yet strangely enough, it was welcomed by untold numbers passing through similar experiences. In gatherings of Christians in New Zealand, however small the informal groups, the name of Professor Blaiklock during those days, often arose. And almost invariably there were one or two who would comment on how much encouragement they had received from the book *Kathleen* when they had been passing through their own bereavements. Oswald Sanders says that during his speaking tours in the United States he often meets people who express themselves similarly about the book.

*Kathleen* was written in daily diary form, not so much of events but of the meanderings of Blaiklock's mind as he admits defeat but tries to face life normally and to act normally. His sensitivity and romanticism are still there – in a more acute form. Does he lose his faith in God? These extracts show him struggling on, holding on:

> *February 17:* The day is done as I sit with the little leather-bound book before me again. Heavy cloud which sometimes comes with an anticyclone has covered the sky all day, putty coloured, depressing. Utter stillness without a moving leaf and pressing hard upon me. I react too strongly to weather and that is true even of two years and more ago, in those now almost unimaginable days of happiness, before the blanket of the dark was spread. I have looked back on what I have written. For whom? Might I harm some? On the other hand, could it be that such frankness might help those who are taunted for their grief and feel that faith is vain if it does not extinguish agony? After all, when we cry in our desolation: 'My God, my God, why hast thou forsaken me?' we are actually quoting Christ.
> 
> *February 5:* I am writing again because she has been strangely with me all day. I have kept her little Honda car, and with the empty seat beside me, I drove across town through Blockhouse Bay . . . I go on, along a route which I cannot abandon, alone. I can say with truth and can say no more, that I carry on as she would wish me to do, doggedly in pain. I speak to the group without faltering, as I did today, and no one knows that I still see a face to my right among them, eyes fixed, a little anxiously on mine.
> 
> *(Extracts)*
> For me there is no new beginning, only left-overs to live.
> I can understand a widower holding battle in contempt and doing heroic deeds because he has no one for whom he really needs to go on living.
> No, I cannot believe that the wonder of conscious life is a ghastly joke played by no one on everyone.

**Dr Alison Blaiklock sums up her reactions to the book on her grandmother.**

> Grandpa received harsh criticism, even abusive letters from those who considered a Christian should not feel as he did. But there were those who recognised the integrity of the book and many found it helpful; he received hundreds of letters from people who felt similarly.
> 
> In general practice patients would notice my surname and say how *Kathleen* put into words the grief they felt – and still felt

perhaps 20 years later for their husband, wife or child. I came to believe that this intense grief that one can only accept but not cure is something relatively common and yet unrecognised or misunderstood both by psychology and those who have not experienced it.

Grandpa had misgivings about writing *Kathleen*. It seemed too private a thing; he was unsure what the reactions would be; he felt he was not being 'the Christian triumphant'. But he decided to tell the story and tell it with openness. It is, I think, his best book, told with love, courage and honesty by a man who keeps going because of his Christian faith.

Despite his deep grief, Blaiklock never gave up as others about his age sometimes do when a partner is lost after long years of happily married life. But he could not escape his grief. When he prayed for relief all he seemed to receive was, 'Keep on praying, keep on asking.'

He kept up his speaking engagements, worked hard at his writings, fulfilled his engagements in Australia and led three more tour parties overseas. These were not the actions of a totally defeated person.

Thanks to family, close friends and particularly some from the Titirangi Presbyterian Church, he found the burden slowly becoming more bearable. That he had regained much of his old composure and the heart of his faith, was demonstrated by the eagerness with which in the last year of his life, he grasped with confidence, a new means (for him) of Christian outreach.

# PART FIVE:
# FACING THE END

## 12  ACTIVE TO THE LAST

Blaiklock had made a number of visits to Australia in earlier years. From 1980–1982 he was to make five more. Australians generally regard New Zealanders as junior colonial brothers or little cousins and there is always the keenest rivalry between them. Blaiklock always enjoyed taking part in the national pastime of belittling his country's next door neighbours. According to Mrs Warwick, who organised his speaking engagements and promoted his books through the Marella Mission, Blaiklock delighted in referring jocularly to Australia as 'New Zealand's offshore island.'

Of his last five visits she writes: 'He had visited the "island Continent" previously for speaking engagements at Katoomba (New South Wales) and Belgrave Heights (Victoria) Christian Conventions. In his five visits between 1980–82, he travelled thousands of kilometres to address Church meetings and business groups, give live radio talks and appear on television.'

Marella Mission, on the north-western outskirts of Sydney, became his base. He enjoyed the rural surroundings, bird life and glorious sunsets. He loved Australia and Sydney for its character. Crossing the Blue Mountains west of Sydney had great fascination for him and he based one of his sermons on 'Going by the Ridges'. Mrs Warwick continues:

> He spoke at St Andrews Anglican Cathedral and St Stephens Uniting Church in the centre of Sydney. He addressed students in universities, theological colleges and schools. In 1982 he had a weekend of meetings in Newcastle. Returning to Sydney he gave an inspiring talk to a large gathering of senior citizens at the Anglican Retirement Villages in Castle Hill, on coming to terms with old age.

The highlight of his ministry in Australia was his participation in an Easter 1982 mission at Trinity Grammar School, Sydney. He lived at the school for several days and proved that though nearly 80 years of age, he still had an excellent rapport with young people. At the mission, the Professor spoke to a meeting of parents, the Crusader group, three large public rallies and by courtesy of the Australian Broadcasting Corporation, gave the address during an across-the-nation Palm Sunday broadcast service.

His main ministry was, however, to the boys – about 900 of them. He talked to them at special Easter services in the school's large assembly hall and in classes, including senior Latin. A divinity class insisted he be fetched from a rest period to talk to them. He found it tiring but exhilarating, the boys exhilarating.

Early in 1983, Blaiklock was approached about having a series of his talks recorded on video tape for possible television viewing and distribution in cassette form. This came about through the initiative of the daughter of Ward Campbell, founder of the Titirangi Presbyterian Church with whom Blaiklock had collaborated closely from the days when he and Kathleen first moved to Koromiko Road.

Althea Campbell had recently returned from twenty-six years missionary work in Kinshasa, Zaire (including also a brief period in Kenya), where she had been involved in radio and television productions as well as in general publication work.

As a cousin of my late wife (she had also been a Campbell), Althea had always looked on our place as her second home. She had lived with us for most of the five years we had spent in the Belgian Congo (now Zaire) in the second half of the 1950s.

On returning home and finding my son and I involved in video and television productions, she urged us to consider doing a series with Professor Blaiklock. 'He can't have too much time left,' she remarked.

At that time Blaiklock was conducting a monthly Bible study based on John's gospel and held every second Tuesday morning at ten o'clock in the Presbyterian Church at Titirangi. There was an average attendance of about fifty, coming from many different parts of the city and representative of different denominations.

Blaiklock could see the potential for videos, and the possibility that his spoken ministry could continue after his death delighted him. 'There is one serious problem, however,' he said. 'I have a lump in my abdomen and I'm not sure what it is. I may not have too much time left.'

He had felt tired during the summer of that year. This he attributed to being what could be expected at eighty years of age and he was irritated that he could no longer take long walks or collect loads of firewood from the bush.

The surgeon confirmed his suspicions. It was cancer of the bowel. There was no evidence of secondary spread, he believed, so it seemed possible, even likely, that an operation could cure him.

It was decided to proceed with a trial programme for the video series and filming for it was done in his study at Koromiko Road on Friday 17 June. To follow this programme, a series of five others had been carefully worked out. The aim was to highlight a classical scholar talking about life and death based on the first eighteen verses of the first chapter of John's gospel. As producer, Althea Campbell worked long hours on the programmes, seeking how best to reveal his scholarship to greatest advantage.

In the first programme, *Why I Believe in God*, Blaiklock was at his best in oratory, descriptive powers and subject matter. Age was no disadvantage and his self-confidence seemed to have returned in full. It was a brilliant fifteen-minute talk in which he demonstrated his scholarship in a relaxed and authoritative manner. It was a trial run for the series, and was so highly commended by those to whom it was shown that it was decided to proceed with the series.

The filming of the first programme took several hours and wearied Blaiklock greatly. That evening he spoke to a meeting in the city on archaeology and had to sit down for most of his talk. He had never felt so physically exhausted since his duodenal operation.

Granddaughter Alison takes up the story:

Grandpa entered the Mater Misericordiae Hospital on Monday, June 21, for an operation the next day. Some of the nuns there were friends and former students and he had long felt an affinity with the traditions and solace found in the Roman Catholic Church.

My brother John and I stayed with him the morning of his operation. Grandpa talked with us about what was in the newspaper, of the love and support he had from family and friends. He was intensely interested in what was happening (he had always been fascinated by medicine) and asked many questions.

When he had his premedication he found that, like many people, he disliked how the drugs affected his clarity of thought so he fought it by making complex conversation. When his surgeon came, he told him he wished he could watch the operation – 'maybe by video?'

The tumour was removed but there was found the beginning of secondary spread in the liver. It was not until several days afterwards he was sufficiently free of pain and the post-operative exhaustion to ask his prognosis. He had insisted we were to tell him the truth. Dad (son Peter) told him directly. Grandpa thanked him.

Blaiklock agreed to visits from his close friends as soon as he was over the worst effects of his operation. One of these was David Stewart. He intended calling in for a few moments only. Blaiklock wanted to talk and Stewart remained for over an hour. 'I've known a great deal of love,' he said to the Bible College principal. 'I have the assurance I have maintained the faith. I have peace I will be going home to God. But I have no joy. I haven't known joy for years.'

Stewart pointed out Christ's use of the word *'emos'* meaning 'my', as recorded in John's gospel. This Greek word is used by Jesus only three times and in each case it is a slightly more emphatic and distinctive way of qualifying the noun which follows. For example,

> My (*emos*) *peace* I leave with you
> Abide in my (*emos*) *love*
> My (*emos*) *joy* I give unto you.

Blaiklock was the Greek scholar with an international reputation. He knew the gospel of John by heart in Greek. Yet in his hour of great need, it was another who ministered to him from the gospel he knew so intimately and loved so much.

Stewart continued that Christ had used the distinctive emphasis for the personal pronoun 'my' in the upper room at a time when he was facing imminent death by crucifixion. 'I can't imagine that was frivolous "peace, joy or love" Christ was talking about,' Stewart said. 'The joy I think Christ meant was probably that which comes from the depth of acceptance – one that can be experienced even in grief.'

Blaiklock appreciated the words Stewart spoke. They struck a chord within him. As Stewart observes:

> He never commented about them to me but in a Grammaticus article a few weeks later, quoting from C. S. Lewis, Blaiklock wrote about being 'surprised by joy'. I have not the slightest doubt it was in response to our talk.
>
> I believe it represented a turning point for him and prepared him for the end. In the last days he had a quiet assurance that the things he had always believed were real. I think that comes out most clearly in the television series he was producing at the time.

After hospital, Blaiklock stayed with a friend during convalescence. She had been a hospital matron and was marvellous to him. 'Grandpa was blessed in his friends,' continues Alison.

> He treasured friendship and his friends responded to his illness by rallying round him. He returned home for the waiting. He knew his time was limited to a matter of months but resolved to keep working as much as he could. He organised his papers, made sure Dad and David understood the details of his affairs (he told me where things were in case, in their grief after his death, Dad and David could not remember where an important document was).

He was keen to do as many of the video programmes he had time for. But now he viewed them differently. He changed the basis of the series, deciding on his own not to keep to the first eighteen verses of the first chapter of John, but to range at will through the gospel.

His second programme, *Why I am not Afraid to Die*, was up to the standard of his first. Now knowing for certain that, at best, he had only months to live gave it additional impact.

Blaiklock was able to fit in five of the six programmes originally planned. But for the remaining three, instead of the classical scholar of international repute, he adopted the role of a local evangelist, with subject matter little different from what one would expect from such a source. There was little in the last three programmes that effectively portrayed him as a scholar. As a result, the possibility of the programmes having an immediate worldwide appeal, was lost. They became just another religious series.

When Blaiklock's literary agent Ray Richards viewed the last three of the video programmes, he says that for the first time with Blaiklock he caught something of a fundamentalist approach. Reviewing the series in the *Listener* of 18 August 1984, journalist Vernon Wright described Blaiklock as 'a Christian fundamentalist'. It was not an appellation Blaiklock would ever have given himself.

For the two Christian young men who comprised the camera team, the days filming the series were ones they looked forward to. Blaiklock was certainly freer in himself than he had been before he had known what 'the lump inside me' was. He almost seemed as if the knowledge that death was just ahead for him had brought a release of spirit.

He was under much less tension than before his operation and he talked freely and fully with the camera team, when not actually filming, about his Christian faith and experiences. He told them how in one of his publications he had written that Luke had died in Rome. He knew this was wrong but had overlooked it in the proofs. Another classical scholar saw his mistake and wrote about it in one of his publications. 'The whole world knew of my mistake,' said Blaiklock. He said he felt humiliated but there was nothing he could do about it.

Later, however, he did have an opportunity. He noticed in the writings of the scholar who had written about his mistake an error in his description of the Acropolis. 'I was very much tempted to get my own back and write about his error but I resisted and have never mentioned it to anyone until now,' he said with a satisfied smile. And he didn't name the other scholar.

Blaiklock had no fear about dying but he feared how he might die. We talked together often and almost casually about his coming death. One of his remarks was: 'Death is like someone waiting in the bush further down the road to jump out on one unexpectedly.' He was particularly concerned in case he should lose his memory before dying. Perhaps this was why about this time, in casual conversation with a neighbour about their school days, he repeated – to her utter astonishment – the names of every boy who had been in his third form at Auckland Grammar School sixty-seven years before!

The Augustani had their final meeting with Blaiklock on a sunny day in the spring of his final year, just weeks before his death. Those at this meeting were: Bruce Baker, Janice and Hugh Cheeseman, Mary and Michael Farrell, Vivienne and Evan Gray, Dianne Ritchie, John and Karen Staniland. Michael Stevens was now permanently in England.

Vivienne Gray recalls:

> We were a varied collection of individuals, even in student days and by now, this fellowship was all some of us had in common. But the bonds of student days can be surprisingly strong. At least we were a cohesive group in the presence of the Professor. Our Associate Professor Crawley, was also present that day to seal the bond.
>
> I asked the Professor when he arrived, whether he could manage the flight of steps leading to the main room. What I got for perhaps my exaggerated concern was a look of amused offence. He took the stairs deliberately and unaided, pausing only at the top to hand me his hat. I should have known.
>
> From the room we met in, there was a clear view across to his house in Titirangi in the west. The atmosphere that day was charged with emotion. He made it easy for us at first, speaking about the progress of his illness unemotionally and telling us quite plainly how near death he was. His apparently philo-

sophical acceptance of death was joined with a very human sadness at having to say goodbye to those he now considered his friends. He left with a few carefully chosen words expressing his emotion, and we responded.

While being driven home, he said he regretted his display of emotion, perhaps thinking it undignified; we appreciated it as a token of his true feeling. We took a group photograph that day, as was customary. He stands at the right edge of the group, turning slightly toward us but looking directly at the camera. His pose suggests he felt close to us and wanted it recorded.

Althea Campbell and I visited him just two weeks and a day before he died. We had set the date to film number six in the video series. But it was now too late. A slight slur in his speech was already noticeable.

He was in his dressing gown when we arrived and we were ushered into the lounge instead of the study, as had been usual. Instead of the camera, we recorded the conversation with him on a hired reel to reel tape recorder.

We asked him if he had gone through periods in his life when he had doubted his faith. He replied:

> I don't think it is possible to have faith without assaults of doubt upon it because faith is not simple credulity, starry-eyed acceptance of everything one is told. Of course one is bound to have doubts and then one goes back to the beginning – and how often have I done that – and thinks it through again from what we said in our first video programme: 'In the beginning was an Intelligence which expressed itself. How did it express itself? It did so in the more and more inexplicable sights of creation and then in the necessary conjunction of God expressing himself in human terms in Christ.'
>
> I've gone over that again and again and again. As I look back at the whole pattern of life I find there is more or less a plan, something worked out beyond my own devising, something that shows itself and manifests itself only over periods where you can see the guiding touch here, the inexplicable intervention there and so on. It is a life of faith diversified by doubt, as Browning puts it in 'Bishop Blougram's Apology', rather than a life of doubt diversified by faith. Anyone who says he has never doubted, I wonder whether he has ever thought.

During our discussion the telephone rang. With a nod from him I answered it. The phone was in the kitchen. A lady wanted to know if she could speak to Blaiklock. I explained this was impossible as he was far from well. Could she come and see him? I thought this also would be impossible but if she would give me her name I would ask him. 'Don't put her off,' Blaiklock said. 'You won't be here very much longer, will you? Tell her to come in a quarter of an hour. I have already talked with her and I think I can help her.'

Before leaving his home, we had, as usual, a short time of prayer. The whole atmosphere was emotionally charged. I had a conviction it was the last time we would see him. My words of prayer just before leaving were uttered haltingly and with large gaps between. He didn't show any emotion but he fully accepted that the brief video production period in his life was now at an end.

As we turned on to Koromiko Road from the Blaiklock driveway, the lady who had telephoned, waited in her small car to drive up to the house.

Later Blaiklock talked with John Rymer, about how he would like a brief and dignified funeral. He wanted it to be at Holy Trinity Cathedral because he had great affection for both the cathedral and the Dean. He realised many people would want to come and he wanted them to be comfortable, to be able to sit down out of the rain.

He went to as many of his speaking engagements as possible. He kept on writing, struggling with a translation of St Francis which he knew he could not finish; two weeks before his death he wrote to his publishers expressing his regret, his apologies that 'I cannot get to the University library to check the original sources,' and his appreciation to them.

*The Little Flowers of St Francis*, published after his death, was his last writing effort. It was completed by his University of Auckland friend, Professor A C Keys, and published by Hodder and Stoughton. It was a task he had been glad to take on but not one in which he found enjoyment. He found, with regret, that St Francis was unable to accept the fullness of Christ's atonement.

In what were possibly the final words written in his own handwriting, he expressed his regrets as being unable to complete his task. On 12 October 1983, just fourteen days before he died, he wrote:

> I confess to some inability to find the gladness in the first members of the Order, which some splendid Franciscans in the Roman Catholic and Anglican Churches seem to find today. Preaching naked in the street was not calculated to honour Christ nor to force a brother to do so in the name of his oath of obedience, was notably Christian. Such matters apart, it has been good to keep a legend of corpus alive (or to join the band who have sought to do so in several modern languages) and like Bede, in AD 735, one of England's first classical scholars, I lay down my pen. Francis has not, I fear, cheered my closing days.

As his bodily weakness increased, his thoughts turned more and more to his approaching death. In conversation with granddaughter Alison, he asked her how he would die and what would be the probable cause of death. Alison remembers:

> I answered him as much as I knew. Honesty was very important. As a family we wanted to look after him when the time came and we talked about this also. Grandpa wanted to be as independent as possible for as long as possible.
> Despite all his determined efforts to look after himself and to keep working, in mid-October, as the cancer spread through his liver, he became too fatigued to get up. His condition deteriorated suddenly – I think he must have had a clot in the lungs – and we thought he was going to die that weekend. Then he improved but the effects of that episode, presumably due to a period of lack of oxygen, were that his kidneys stopped working.
> Dad retired from his work just before this and stayed with Grandpa. We were fortunate because most of the family were able to take annual leave or work glide-time so as to be able to look after Grandpa. We were fortunate again because in the family there are three nurses (who taught the rest of us some skills), an occupational therapist and two doctors.
> Not only were his friends supportive but there were also the

district nurses who came once or twice daily as well as the Cancer Society, who sent a nurse every night so people could sleep.

Hence we were able to do what many people long to do but are unable for very practical reasons; to look after Grandpa in his own home, surrounded by his family and the kauri trees outside his bedroom windows, until he died.

As he drifted in and out of a coma, he would sometimes speak in Latin or Greek. But what he said that we could understand was always appreciative and courteous. When we turned him he would struggle to help and thank us. When we cleaned his teeth his eyes would show great love. He told us: 'I'm going to be with Kathleen (he had chosen to sleep in Kathleen's bed for his last days), and that 'if this is dying, it's quite easy'.

Grandpa's last words before his final coma were when the night nurse said she was going to get Ken to help turn him. Ken was sleeping in the library because it now required two people to turn Grandpa without pain. He said: 'Don't wake Ken, let him sleep'.

So he died with dignity, without fear, loving and beloved. It was October 26, 1983.

When talking with Alison shortly before the diagnosis of Blaiklock's terminal illness, Dr L K Gluckman, an eminent psychiatrist and scholar, had remarked: 'He is the last of the Romans.'

The 'Letters to the Editor' columns of the *New Zealand Herald* were full of testimonials to the impact of his Grammaticus writings for days after Blaiklock's death. Others spoke of the counsel and advice they had received when they had communicated with him following something that had moved them in his writings. (A book entitled *The Best of Grammaticus* published after his death sold all its 5000 copies in New Zealand in a few weeks.)

The story of a nonagenarian patient, John Ritchie, whom David was seeing every three months had fascinated Blaiklock, particularly his experiences as a soldier in Gallipoli with the Anzacs in the First World War. Out of respect to his long life and military service, David would rise and salute him each time he came to the surgery. At his first visit after Blaiklock's death, David followed his usual custom. Ritchie merely put out his hand and with great emotion, said, 'A great man has gone home.'

There was not one vacant seat in the Cathedral for the funeral service at 2 p.m. on Saturday, 29 October. An hour before the service the rain poured down in torrents, during the service and for an hour following.

Dean Rymer spoke of the last moments he had had with Blaiklock at his bedside:

> When I asked him what meaning he had made of life, he answered me in a biblical text, 'All things work to a pattern of good to them that love God.'
> Then I asked him how he felt at the present moment, knowing he was about to die. He said: 'I've really left this world. It is as though I were in a departure lounge of an airport. The 747 is warming up in the lower tarmac and before long it will take me to my final destination. I wonder what company there will be there with me.'
> And then I said: 'Well, what about beyond death?' He replied: 'My greatest hope is to be reunited with Kathleen but over and above that I want to hear from God that my life has been worthwhile. I find I have tried to fight a good fight – at times perhaps not very well but wouldn't it be wonderful if there is a crown of righteousness laid up in heaven for me?'
> We talked a little more, then said our final prayers and bade one another farewell. But as I left the house, I realised that in his mind, he was indeed journeying with St Paul, where the latter said in 2 Timothy 4:6:
>
>> For I am now ready to be offered, and the time of my departure is at hand. I have fought a good fight, I have finished my course, I have kept the faith: henceforth there is laid up for me a crown of righteousness, which the Lord, the righteous judge, shall give me at that day: and not to me only, but unto all them also that love his appearing.
>
> As I went further down the hill, I knew that what this scholar had said so often with his lips was embedded in his heart and mind, that that was the sustenance taking him to eternity.

The finality of Blaiklock's life hit the family, to use David's own words, 'as I turned and walked out of the crematorium; and yet I sensed very much he was still alive. In his library, a table at which he had been working held a dictionary of the Christian Church. On top of it was an open pair of spectacles. It was as though he had just got up and gone.'

Among his papers, to be opened after his death, was a message for his family. It had been written in his own handwriting and was dated 16 August 1982. It read:

> If by some turn of circumstance you should not see me again, remember, dear ones, that it is 'glory for me', waiting ended and all I have lost regained. Tell the grandchildren to keep the faith, or, if they have lost it, to seek and find it again. I have proved it in joy and agony of mind. There is no other way by which to make any sense of life. Agnosticism is not a way of life. No snatching at imaginary advantage brings peace of mind. Choose no way of death.
>
> If it is in any way possible to press for good upon the lives of all of you from some other state of being, I will do so as I can.
>
> Live life well. It gives its best to the brave, the loyal, the gentle, the true, the clean. Wandering brings no peace. God bless you all and may life end for you in due time without unhappiness, loneliness and pain. Fight through your problems, never turn from one another and always remember that failure is not final.
> – Grandpa.

A few days later it was discovered that the plum tree at Wood Bay, which had grown from a stone casually thrown when Blaiklock and Cliff Mitchell had camped there as young men and which later became for Blaiklock and Kathleen a living memorial to her brother's martyrdom in Abyssinia in 1955, had been struck by lightning during the electrical storm over Auckland which had coincided with Blaiklock's funeral service in the Auckland Cathedral.

# EPILOGUE

My earliest memory of Edward Musgrave Blaiklock was when I was one of a large church audience held enthralled by his skill with words and the impact of his message. Fifty years later, just weeks before he died, it was still an uplifting experience to attend his monthly, hour-long lectures with 40–50 others in the Titirangi Presbyterian Church.

This was Blaiklock's genius – his ability to breathe new life into old truths. In any gathering in which he was present, one found it impossible to resist the shock waves of his discourse or oratory. It was this gift, based on his vast storehouse of knowledge, that endeared him to thousands.

As the inspired communicator, Blaiklock made history and the Bible comprehensible and relevant to his day. Theologically he was an apologist, politically and socially a conservative.

His conservatism was born in the days on the Titirangi farm with his father, whose pioneering and risk-taking ended in failure. For the son, therefore, these paths in life were to be avoided. The things that were overwhelmingly important to Blaiklock were financial security, social status and (reemphasized following his conversion experience), personal integrity.

Blaiklock's conversion did not follow a long period of inner struggle and did not make a major change in his daily living. The issues he had to face after conversion were in the intellectual and literary arenas. On a personal level, his faith was rarely severely tested until later in life.

For example, during the world's most violent century, the personal tragedies and traumas which so many experienced, did not touch Blaiklock personally. He was not involved as an active serviceman in either of the two world wars and during the depression of the 1930s, he had job security, a mortgage free home and a happy marriage dominated by love, stability and permanence.

I remember consulting Blaiklock on how I should counsel a family in the midst of very deep personal suffering. It was in the early days of the 1960s and I was pastor (for a temporary period) of the Hillsborough Baptist Church in Auckland. Blaiklock was taking a 13-week series of Sunday morning pulpit addresses in the church. He replied that as he had never known personal suffering, he was not able to advise me.

As a result of the favourable circumstances in which Blaiklock and Kathleen shared a full and contented life together, they were largely confined within a fortress wall of isolation from the struggles and crises faced by many others. Thus when Kathleen died, Blaiklock found his faith totally inadequate for the crisis.

His emotional flood gates opened and he became adrift on mountainous seas of grief. By a slender thread he clung to faith in God and finally, before having to face his own death, found his faith strengthened by the experience.

His last words epitomised the victory for all those who embrace (often in hesitancy, weaknesses and many failures) the life of faith.

> If this is death, there
> is nothing to fear.

# APPENDIX 1: PROFESSOR BLAIKLOCK'S TELEVISION SERIES

A six-part television series, 'A Mind Behind It All,' was prepared with Professor Blaiklock in the last year of his life. The series, produced by Vision Videos Society Ltd, P.O. Box 39–203, Auckland West, appeared on New Zealand Televison One, following his death.

*PART ONE*: The Professor is introduced to the series by the Dean of St Mary's Cathedral, Auckland, the Most Rev John Rymer. The Dean speaks of the relationship between the Professor's faith and his scholarship.

*PART TWO*: Using illustrations from nature, Professor Blaiklock expounds his belief that there is a mind behind creation. 'In the beginning was an intelligence, a mind which expressed itself.' In the objects around them, people can distinguish between the products of mere chance and of intelligent creativity.

*PART THREE*: Suddenly confronted with the knowledge that he has only a few weeks to live, Professor Blaiklock affirms, as an historian as well as a Christian, his belief in the resurrection of Christ, testing the gospel story by academic investigation.

*PART FOUR*: The existence of a vast intelligence around us has been demonstrated but it would be very daunting if we could not make contact with it. So it was necessary to have the second revelation in Jesus Christ his Son – he was God, the Word, translating himself into a language that we could understand.

*PART FIVE*: Why did not the authorities arrest Jesus for a breach of the peace when he 'drove the animals out of the temple . . . overturned the tables of the money changers'?

APPENDIX 1

The very presence of Christ is irresistible, be it in the temple become a market place or in the clutter of our own lives.

*PART SIX*: An English philosopher once argued that anything that can't be seen, heard, felt or smelt, does not exist. The evidence of a mind at work in creation does not necessarily enable us to picture that person. We must therefore look at his Son to see God's attributes – his wrath against hypocrisy and sham; his impatience, his patience and his love.

The video series is distributed by the following in cassette form:

NEW ZEALAND: ESTV, P.O. Box 41018, Eastbourne, Wellington.

AUSTRALIA: Australian Religious Film Society, P.O. Box 97 North Ryde, N.S.W. 2133.

UNITED STATES: Gateway Films, Box A, Lonsdale, Pennsylvania 19446.

GREAT BRITAIN: Bagster Video, Westbrook House, 76 High Street, Alton, Hampshire GU34 1EN.

# APPENDIX 2:   BIBLIOGRAPHY

Published book titles bearing the name of Professor Blaiklock are listed herewith. He was sole author of the following publications unless otherwise stated as co-author, editor, contributing editor or contributor:

| | | |
|---|---|---|
| 1947 | *Two Letters from Prison* (Philippians & Philemon) | Institute Press (Reprinted 1964, Pickering & Inglis as *From Prison in Rome*). |
| 1947 | *The Way of Excellence* (1 Cor. 13 & Romans 12) | Institute Press (Reprinted 1968 by Pickering & Inglis) |
| 1947 | *Read it Again* | Institute Press |
| 1948 | *The Decline and Fall of the Athenian Democracy* | University of Auckland |
| 1949 | *Medical Personalities of the Ancient World* | Royal Australian College of Physicians |
| 1949 | *No Mists Above* | Institute Press (Reprinted 1966) |
| 1952 | *The Male Characters of Euripides* | University of New Zealand |
| 1952 | *The Seven Churches* (Revelation 2–3) | Marshall, Morgan and Scott |
| 1952 | *Not Made to Die* | Institute Press |
| 1957 | *Out of the Earth* (Archaeology and the New Testament) | Wm B Erdmanns – Revised, enlarged, republished 1961, Paternoster Press |
| 1958 | *The Romanticism of Catullus* | University of Auckland |
| 1958 | *The Christian in Pagan Society* | Inter-Varsity Press |

| | | |
|---|---|---|
| 1959 | *The Epistles of John* | Paternoster Press, republished as *Faith is the Victory*, Regal Books 1975, and *Letters to the Children of Light*, 1981. |
| 1959 | *Rome In the New Testament* | Inter-Varsity Press |
| 1959 | *Acts – The Birth of the Church* | Inter-Varsity Fellowship Press; republished 1980, Fleming H Revell. |
| 1960 | *The Hero of Aeneid* | University of Auckland. |
| 1962 | *Pictorial Bible Dictionary* – Contributor | Zondervan Publishing House |
| 1964 | *The Areopagus Address* | Rendle Short Memorial Lecture, Bristol. |
| 1964 | *Our Lord's Teaching on Prayer* | Oliphants; reprinted 1974, Regal Books, as *The Positive Power of Prayer* |
| 1965 | *Ten Pounds an Acre* | A H and A W Reed |
| 1965 | *The Century of the New Testament* | Inter-Varsity Press |
| 1965 | *Cities of the New Testament* | Pickering and Inglis |
| 1966 | *Mark: The Man and his Message* | Paternoster Press |
| 1966 | *Understanding the New Testament* *Romans* – Study Book *Luke* – Study Book | Scripture Union (Both books reprinted, 1978) |
| 1966 | *Hills of Home* | A H and A W Reed |
| 1966 | *The Roman and his Trouble* | University of Auckland |
| 1967 | *Dictionary of Practical Theology* – Contributor | Wm B Erdmanns |
| 1967 | *Green Shades* | A H and A W Reed |
| 1967 | *In the Image of Peter* | Paternoster Press and Moody Press |

| | | |
|---|---|---|
| 1968 | *The Way of Excellence* (Romans 12 and 1 Cor. 13) | Pickering and Inglis |
| 1968 | *Cicero on Old Age* | University of Auckland |
| 1968 | *Is It or Isn't It?* – Co-author | Zondervan Publishing House. Printed also in German and Chinese, Reprinted 1972, 76 as *Why Didn't They Tell Me?* |
| 1968 | *Layman's Answer* | Hodder and Stoughton and Judson Press |
| 1969 | *Pictorial Bible Atlas* – Contributor | Zondervan Publishing House |
| 1970 | *The Archaeology of the New Testament* | Zondervan Publishing House. Reprinted 1974 |
| 1970 | *The Psalms of the Great Rebellion* | Marshall, Morgan and Scott |
| 1970 | *Apostolic History and the Gospel* | Paternoster Press |
| 1971 | *Word Pictures from the Bible* – Contributor | Zondervan Publishing House and Pickering and Inglis |
| 1971 | *Why I am Still a Christian* – Contributing editor | Zondervan Publishing House |
| 1972 | *The Pastoral Epistles* | Zondervan Publishing House |
| 1973 | *Bible Characters and Doctrines* – Co-author | Scripture Union and Wm B Erdmanns |
| 1974 | *Who was Jesus?* | Moody Press. Reprinted 1983, Anzea Publishers as *Man or Myth?*, also 1984, Thomas Nelson |
| 1974 | *Epistles of John* | Paternoster and Regal |
| 1975 | *New Testament Studies* – Contributor | Baylor University Press |
| 1975 | *The Bible in our World* | Bible Society, Australia – Oliver Beguin Lecture |

| | | |
|---|---|---|
| 1977 | *Commentary on the New Testament* | Hodder & Stoughton |
| 1977 | *First Peter* – translation and devotional commentary | Word Books |
| 1977 | *Psalms for Living* – Vol 1, 1–72 | Scripture Union |
| 1977 | *Psalms for Worship* – Vol 2, 73–150 | Scripture Union |
| 1978 | *The Answer's in the Bible* | Hodder & Stoughton |
| 1979 | *The Imitation of Christ* – Thomas à Kempis, a fresh translation and introduction | Hodder & Stoughton |
| 1979 | *The World of the Middle East* | Christian Literature Crusade. Reprinted 1981 as *The World of the New Testament* |
| 1979 | *Meditation on the Psalms* Four books:   1–37            38–75            76–111            112–150 | Scripture Union. Republished in one volume 1985 as *Living Waters* |
| 1979 | *Handbook of Bible People* – 740 studies of Bible characters | Scripture Union |
| 1979 | *Between the Valley and the Sea* – autobiographical | Dunmore Press |
| 1979 | *Kathleen – The Record of a Sorrow* | Hodder & Stoughton |
| 1979 | *New International Version of the Bible* – Revising editor | Hodder & Stoughton |
| 1979 | *New King James Version* – Contributor and revising editor | Thomas Nelson |
| 1980 | *Between the Morning and the Afternoon* (autobiographical) | Dunmore Press |

| | | |
|---|---|---|
| 1980 | *Blaiklock's Bible Handbook* (companion vol. to Commentary on the New Testament) | Hodder & Stoughton |
| 1980 | *Illustrated Bible Dictionary* (in three volumes) – Contributor | Hodder & Stoughton |
| 1980 | *Daily Thoughts from Keswick* – Contributor | Hodder & Stoughton |
| 1980 | *Still a Christian* | Hodder & Stoughton |
| 1980 | *Eight Days in Israel* | Ark Press |
| 1981 | *Between the Foothills and the Ridge* (autobiographical) | Dunmore Press |
| 1981 | *Brother Lawrence – Practice of the Presence of God* (a translation) | Hodder & Stoughton – Thomas Nelson |
| 1982 | *A Love of Trees* | Dunmore Press |
| 1982 | *Between the Sunset and the Stars* | Hodder & Stoughton |
| 1983 | *Six Weeks to Eternity* | Anzea Publishers |
| 1983 | *The Bible and I* (autobiographical) | Marshall, Morgan & Scott |
| 1983 | *The Confessions of St Augustine* – a translation | Hodder & Stoughton |
| 1983 | *Dictionary of Biblical Archaeology* | Zondervan Publishing House |
| 1984 | *The Best of Grammaticus* | Wilson & Horton |
| 1985 | *The Little Flowers of St Francis* – co-author | Hodder & Stoughton |